BARNABAS

ENCOURAGING EXHORTER

A STUDY IN MENTORING

Bobby Clinton
Laura Raab

ISBN 1-932814-20-5

Barnabas Publishers

P.O. Box 6006
Altadena, CA 91003-6006

Printed in The United States of America

Cover Design, Cover Illustration and Book Layout by D. M. Battermann
Word-Processing by R. D. Battermann

Table of Contents

Appendices

Appendices A-2 through A-12 are copied from Bobby Clinton's book *Spiritual Gifts* and used by permission. Appendix A-1, A-13 through A-19 are copied from Bobby Clinton's *Leadership Emergence Theory* and used by permission.

PREFACE

This book is one of a series of leadership biographical studies. Leadership is a life-time process in which God interacts in the life of a leader to,

- point out potential for leadership (focuses on integrity),
- develop that potential in the leader,
- guide that leader into service, and
- use that leader for His own purposes.

A leader may be born with potential to lead, but it is God who processes that leader so that the potential is realized. Opportunities, experience and training (formal, non-formal and informal) all combine with giftedness to make a leader. And God is active in the whole process.

The major events, people, circumstances, crises, etc. through which God works to develop, guide and use a leader are called process items. The ideas of leadership selection and process items are described in Bobby Clinton's self-study text called *Leadership Emergence Theory*. Definitions of process items from that book which apply to this study are included in an appendix at the end of this study. The *Leadership Emergence Theory* book is available through Barnabas Publishers.

Study Summary

Person Studied: Barnabas

Direct Data:

Acts 4:32-37	giftedness; expectation (Jerusalem)
Acts 9:23-31	linker – Paul (Jerusalem)
Acts 11:22-26	linker – Antioch (Antioch)
Acts 12:25-13:5	linker – Paul to apostolic function (Antioch)
Acts 13:6-16	cross-cultural mission (Cyprus, et al)
Acts 14:8-20	contextualization (Lystra/Lycaonia)
Acts 15:1-35	linker – contextualization conflict
Acts 15:36-41	conflict – mentor disengagement (Antioch)

Indirect Data:

Gal. 1:11-19	linking Paul (Jerusalem)
Gal. 2:1-10	apostolic confirmation (Jerusalem)
Gal. 2:11-14	apostolic conflict (Antioch)
Col. 4:10	family factor
1 Cor. 9:6	sphere of influence

Abbreviated Time Line

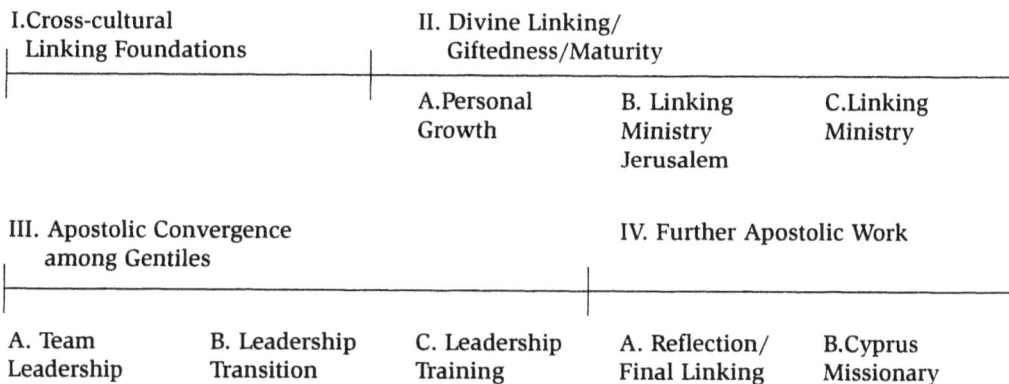

I.Cross-cultural Linking Foundations		II. Divine Linking/ Giftedness/Maturity		
		A.Personal Growth	B. Linking Ministry Jerusalem	C.Linking Ministry

III. Apostolic Convergence among Gentiles			IV. Further Apostolic Work	
A. Team Leadership	B. Leadership Transition	C. Leadership Training	A. Reflection/ Final Linking	B.Cyprus Missionary

Gift-Mix: **exhortation**, apostleship, teaching, (evangelism)

Sphere of influence: direct – small national (Island – Cyprus)
indirect – international through mentoree – Paul

Major Contributions:

1. As a mentor, Barnabas linked Christianity into the Gentile world. It is probably fair to say that without Barnabas, Christianity would be only one of the many variations of Judaism and still contained in Jewish circles.

2. He functioned as a mentor for Paul and John Mark. He linked Paul to the power base of Christianity on Jerusalem. He further linked Paul to a ministry-growth experience at Antioch from which would come his apostolic recognition. He also linked the new form of Christianity back to Jerusalem. He played a major role in developing John Mark. The Goodwin expectancy principle is reflected in Barnabas' work with John Mark. His patient mentoring brought out this leader.

3. He is a major New Testament model of the gifts of apostleship and exhortation. The admonition, encouragement and caring thrusts of exhortation are demonstrated in his ministry.

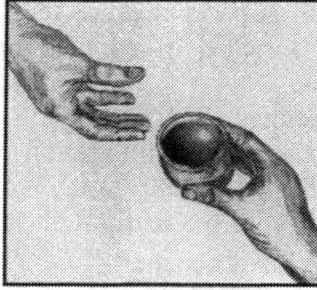

WHY WE CHOSE TO STUDY BARNABAS

Interest

Barnabas is a most underrated contributor to the spread of New Testament Christianity. In today's modern athletic world, he would be one of those unsung linemen who renegotiates his contract upward to a multi-year multi-million-dollar one. And he would deserve it.

Our interest in studying Barnabas stems from the following major sources:

1. The similarities between my own gift-mix and that of Barnabas. In recent years I have come to see exhortation as my dominant gift and have taken steps to move toward convergence in its use. (Bobby)
2. An article[1] on mentoring done by World Vision focused on Barnabas' key linking role. (Bobby)
3. Dennis Teague[2] did a programmed instruction study manual on the gift of exhortation which used Barnabas as the key illustration of the gift of exhortation. (Bobby)
4. Bobby Clinton talked about Barnabas with such enthusiasm in his Leadership Perspectives class that I was also motivated to study him. (Laura)
5. While I do not see myself in traditional roles of leadership or leadership training, I can see myself in the role of a mentor. Thus, I would like to find out more what this means. (Laura)

---

1. The article was later printed in *Interest* 47 (1. January 1982):7-9, under the title, "On Being a Mentor – How To Be a Servant in a Truly Biblical Sense."

2. Teague was interested in training at the local church level in the French context. He wanted to design study materials for developing spiritual gifts in level 1-and-2 leaders.

Expectations

1. I believe this study will expand my understanding of mentoring and thus be a major step forward in convergence of my own gift-mix. (Bobby, Laura)
2. I hope to develop a biblical illustration of the gift of exhortation. In fact, I hope to develop a biblical illustration of each of the leadership and influence gifts. I find that it is much easier to teach an abstract concept like the definition of a spiritual gift if you can wrap it up in a person. (Bobby)
3. I hope to provide a model (format-wise) for doing a biographical study. (Bobby)
4. I expect that God will use this study of Barnabas to significantly influence others in the area of their personal spiritual formation. (Bobby, Laura)

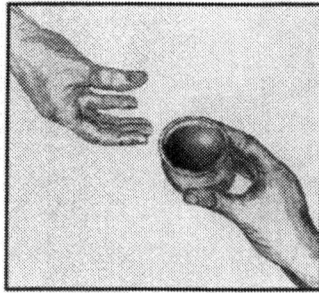

CAPSULE OF BARNABAS

Early Background

Barnabas was a Jewish Levite from Cyprus. His island worldview – including his multi-cultural and maritime exposure – and his network of friends and contacts and his Jewish heritage would all combine uniquely so that he became God's man to link Christianity to a Gentile world.

Barnabas migrated to Jerusalem. It is not clear why he did so. J. A. Robertson suggests that he was a dedicated Levite who studied in Jerusalem and then became a ruler of the synagogue there (1920:46). However, his move to Jerusalem was certainly connected with the fact that he had relatives among the earliest followers of Christ. Barnabas may have encountered Christ in his earthly ministry. Robertson, an imaginative writer, suggests he is the unnamed rich young ruler of the Gospels (1920:46ff). In any case, Barnabas, unnamed in the Gospels, was swept up into "the Way"[3] in its earliest flourishing moments.

Early Christian Growth

The first mention of Barnabas in the Scriptures (Acts 4:36) teems with implications showing growth in his inner-life. This vignette gives us some hints of Barnabas' early background and responses to Christian truth. Barnabas:

  1. was a Jewish Levite from Cyprus (and the Cyprus connection will later

---

3. "The Way" was a descriptive term in Acts designating those early followers of Christ (see Acts 9:2; 19:9,23; 24:14,22; possibly Acts 16:17; 18:25,26). It is significant that it was primarily due to Barnabas' own ministry that a new term, at least among the Gentiles, began to be used: Christians.

be seen to be sovereignly used by God in a major linking function);

2. was a part of the Christian movement while it was vital[4] (growing both in quality and quantity);
3. was early challenged by Christian truth and responded positively to it in sacrificial obedience;
4. learned the freedom of giving early and was able all through life to pass on this essential Christian characteristic;
5. exercised his gift of exhortation in such a way as to encourage others both by his life and words;
6. was recognized by the Jewish leaders as leadership potential;
7. received a name which prophetically set the bent of his life; it was also an expression of Goodwin's expectation principle.[5]

We are introduced to Barnabas as a person sensitive to the Holy Spirit. He is a person of integrity. These observations flow from the fact that Barnabas' early giving example is contrasted with the next which negatively reveals Ananias and Sapphira as people not sensitive to the Spirit and without inner integrity. This early observation of Barnabas as a person of potential sets the stage for observing the realization of potential.

Growth in Sphere of Influence

Barnabas performed his first mentor-linking function when he sponsored Paul to the Jerusalem Christian leaders (Acts 9:23,24). That Paul was accepted by the Jewish Christian leaders is evidence of the growth that had occurred in Barnabas' life. He was respected for his life, ministry and judgment – all signs of spiritual authority.[6] This divine contact[7] with Paul was to be the key to God's expansion of Christianity to a Gentile world.

---

4. It has long been the opinion of church growth scholars that leaders who have never experienced vital growth find it extremely difficult to desire, plan for and expect church growth. Unique strategy designs for training leaders for church growth seek to put in an experiential training component that allows the trainee to be exposed to vital growth situations.

5. Goodwin, in his small paperback book, *The Effective Leader*, identifies the principle which I have modified to apply to leaders. "A potential leader tends to rise to the level of genuine expectancy of a leader he/she respects."

6. Spiritual authority is a technical term used in LET to describe the prime power base of a biblical leader. Lillie's sphere of influence profile is concluded in the appendices. It is a first attempt to reflect power bases (among which is spiritual authority). Spiritual authority is defined on p. 71 of the LET as the characteristic of a God-anointed leader which: a) rests upon clear evidence that Jesus speaks through the leader's life and ministry; b) relates to the influence the leader has on followers for their good; c) is measured by the degree to which believers are yielding and responsive to the leader's persuasive influence; and d) brings about spiritual maturity in those so influenced.

7. Divine contact is a technical term applied to a person whom God brings into the life of a leader at a crucial time in order to influence the leader in one of several ways. See LET p. 49 for a full definition and illustration.

First Major Ministry Task

The Jewish Christian leaders appointed Barnabas to investigate the Antioch manifestation of Christianity. It seems clear that God was working behind the scene to insure that Barnabas was chosen for this task. God used sovereign foundations factors (island worldview, familiarity with Greeks, Cyprus connections), Barnabas' positive growth in ministry and spiritual authority and experiential understanding of Christianity (Cornelius' revelation) to select Barnabas for this apostolic ministry test. He was able to judge the manifestations he saw in light of the word of truth he knew and gave a positive recommendation that this was genuine Christianity. His gifts of apostleship and exhortation were in focus during this visit. He was able to link this Gentile Christianity with the Jewish Christianity at Jerusalem. He built a sound base of relationships at Antioch from which he could correct problems with the Gentile Christianity. Further evidence is given of growth in spiritual authority (it being he was a good man and full of the Holy Spirit and that many people were brought to the Lord – Acts 11:24).

A Major Linking Function

A key apostolic function occurs next. Barnabas saw certain needs in the Antioch church. He remembered Paul's potential. He links Paul to the Antioch church. This co-ministry with Paul would do three major things. It would bring Paul into the mainstream of Christianity, it would develop Paul in ministry gifts and status, and it would build up the Antioch church. The evidence that this did in fact occur is captured in those familiar words, "It was at Antioch that the believers were first called Christians," and in the later words, "In the church at Antioch, there were some prophets and teachers: Barnabas . . . and Saul."

Continued Linking Ministry

Barnabas' heart for giving was passed on to the people of the Antioch church. Their response to Agabus' word of prophecy indicated the reality of that doctrine in their life-styles. This occasion revealed several things. Barnabas discerned that this was indeed a word from the Lord, an apostolic function. He was able to motivate the church to follow this guidance (a leadership function). He was able to link two churches at the regional level more firmly together. And God rewarded this positive response of Barnabas by outward confirmation of a sense of destiny. Barnabas and Paul were recognized by the Jewish Christian leaders as apostles to the Gentiles.

Foundational Linking to Other Gentiles

It is no surprise then that upon their return to Antioch, God gave a new apostolic assignment to Barnabas. Barnabas would bridge Christianity to other Gentiles. At this point Barnabas had evidenced a mature use of the following spiritual gifts: apostleship, teaching and exhortation. There are other indications that mercy and giving were also a part of his gift-mix.[8]Although multi-gifted, his dominant gift was exhortation. His spiritual authority was sound and attested to by the Jewish Christian leaders at Jerusalem as well as the Antioch church in general and the leadership in particular. Barnabas and Paul were released by the church and sent forth by the Holy Spirit for a second crucial ministry task – setting the pattern of expansion of Christianity among the Gentiles. Barnabas, true to his exhortive gift and mentoring experience, took along a protégé, John Mark, who would develop in an informal apprenticeship.

Barnabas' connections to Cyprus made it a natural target for the first planned cross-cultural evangelism. Fundamental lessons on power and the need to contextualize the "unto now Jewish message" were learned in the first evangelistic experience. That churches should be organized out of the evangelistic effort was yet to be learned in the second stage of this apostolic ministry task. Barnabas had co-ministered with Paul for an extended period of time. Paul's leadership potential had reached the point where it must be released. Exactly how this came about is not recorded. However, that it did come about is clearly indicated in the phrase, "Paul and his companions sailed from Paphos and came to Perga." It is clear that John Mark, who signed on with this missionary team under Barnabas (his cousin) as leader, was not happy with the new leadership. He left the team. This conflict process item was to prove an ongoing conflict which would eventually result in "indirect sovereign guidance" in the separation of Paul and Barnabas.

Conflict and Church Pattern Established

The transition to leadership under Paul was made. One of the great expressions of a mentor is seen in Barnabas' reaction to this. He was able to place himself under submission to Paul and to support Paul in his leadership. Barnabas had almost completed his mentoring role with Paul. Together the two learned about the contextualization of the Gospel, the need for power confirmation of the message in new cultures, the need under conflict and pressure to separate believers into autonomous structures, and the need to establish and release leaders to grow into ministry and spiritual authority. This pattern was to become the dominant pattern for cross-cultural ministry by Paul in the rest of his missionary career. Paul's ability to push out theological frontiers in the understanding of truth was evidently confirmed by Barnabas, for together they would journey to the Jerusalem Council. And more importantly, Barnabas would bridge between the "old understanding" and the "new." For he (not Paul) had the credentials in Jerusalem to bridge this back to the Jewish Christianity base.

Further Conflict Leads to Confirmation of Contextualization

Upon completion of the ministry task for which they had been released by

---

8. Gift-mix is a technical term in Leadership Selection Processes (LSP) theory indicating the cluster of gifts seen in a leader.

the church and sent out by the Holy Spirit, the team returned to Antioch. Here they not only reported what had happened but instructed the church in what they themselves had been learning through this experience. Again, conflict from within the church (Jewish Christians with a narrow understanding of Christian truth) threatened to split a large number of regional churches from their ties with the Antioch Christians. This conflict included even Peter. Barnabas, true to his bridging experience, sought to help Peter in the conflict. Paul strongly opposed both and convinced them of the seriousness of what they were modeling. Barnabas and Paul forced an apostolic gathering to resolve the issue. It was at this point that Barnabas performed his final linking function. At the Jerusalem Council, Barnabas who was well known and respected by the Jewish Christians in Jerusalem, again took the lead in bringing out the truth. The confirmation by this apostolic gathering gave final release to Paul, both in content and methodology, to evangelize the Gentile world. Barnabas' linking ministry as a divine contact for Paul was essentially completed.

Indirect Guidance

Barnabas and Paul, upon their return to Antioch, separate over the issue of whether to take John Mark on a return missionary trip. Barnabas, ever the patient, tolerant mentor, sees potential in John Mark which should be developed. Barnabas and John Mark return to Cyprus. We assume that they establish churches there among those converts arising from the first missionary ministry task.

Final Surmising

We hear no more of Barnabas other than two indirect references. In I Corinthians, Paul mentions Barnabas in connection with teaching on apostleship and giving. From this mention three things could be assumed:

1) Barnabas was still involved in ministry,
2) Paul and Barnabas had at least made some bridging of their relationship,
3) Barnabas was using a tentmaking strategy in his apostolic role.

A second mention in Colossians 4:10 shows that Barnabas' work with John Mark was not in vain. His mentoring function, particularly the discernment quality of seeing potential in yet-to-be-developed leaders, was vindicated.

Indirectly we can infer that Barnabas' sphere of influence remained at a small national level (Cyprus), for if he had expanded his ministry, it most likely would have been the evangelization of the other Mediterranean islands. It seems clear that he did not, for Paul addresses his letter to Titus in terms of the island of Crete.

And so Barnabas passes from the pages of the New Testament. He was born into a contextual situation which fitted him to be a natural bridge to the Gentile world. By gifts, training, growth and temperament, he was divinely suited to link Christianity to the Gentile world. His exhortive, apostolic gift-mix was greatly used by God "unto its full measure of faith."[9]

Overview and Detailed Phase Chart:
Phase 1 (Cross-Cultural Linking Foundations)

Time Span	30 + Years	
Biblical Data	Acts 4:36-37 Col 4:10	
Essential Geography	Cyprus	Jerusalem
Context/Events/People		Crucifixion
Major Process Factors/ Detailed Items	Foundational •Family (Levite) •Family (geography/island worldview/Greek) •Family (mobility: either whole family moved or Barnabas went for study) •Family (relatives/network)	
Possible Gift-Mix		
Sphere of Influence	Possibly local synagogue	

---

9. This phrase occurs in the Romans 12 gift context. Faith here is used by metonymy to stand for spiritual gift which is exercised by faith. Measure indicates capacity. The passage admonishes believers to evaluate and use their gifts to the God-intended capacity for which they were given. In my opinion, Barnabas did.

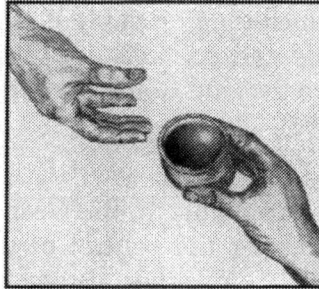

NARRATIVE EXPLANATION OF PHASE I:
CROSS-CULTURAL LINKING FOUNDATIONS

Overview

This development phase probably lasted a minimum of thirty years, since that was considered the age when a Jewish man could begin ministry and since Barnabas was already well respected in the Jerusalem church (as reflected in his being chosen to go to Antioch). It is also possible that he was much older since at Iconium he was identified with Zeus, who is represented in Greek art as a mature figure past the time of middle age (Filson 1940:89).

The focus of this phase is on God's preparation of Barnabas to be a linker, although it is unlikely that Barnabas would have been aware of this at the time.

The major process items in this phase all relate to Barnabas' family background:

1. Family (Levite)
2. Family (geography/island worldview/Greek)
3. Family (mobility)
4. Family (relatives/network)

Process Item I: Family (Levite)

Because Barnabas was a Levite, he had probably been strictly raised in the Jewish tradition. This foundation would later make him a credible choice for the Jerusalem church to send to Antioch. They would trust him to interpret the innovations there in light of his strict Jewish traditions.

Process Item II: Family (Geography/Island Worldview/Greek)

His island worldview – including his multi-cultural and maritime exposure – and his network of friends and contacts and his Jewish heritage would all combine uniquely so that he became God's man to link Christianity to a Gentile world.

The area where Barnabas was born was key in his later ministry. Cyprus had been an island of great importance in the Near East from very early times. From 22 B.C., it had been under the control of the Roman senate and was administered by a proconsul or governor (Bruce 1954:262-63). The myth of Venus Aphrodite was popular there (Ryley 1893:30). Thus Barnabas had exposure both to the Roman way of doing things and to pagan religions.

Because Barnabas was a Jew of the Dispersion, he probably ". . . knew Greek from his early years. He also knew Hellenistic Judaism, and had observed not only its adaptations to life in Gentile lands, but also its attempts to reach Gentiles and gain them as proselytes for the Jewish religion" (Filson 1940:96).

Later Cyprus was the first stop on the missionary journey made by Barnabas and Paul. They could begin their cross-cultural ministry in a setting at least somewhat familiar to Barnabas.

Process Item III: Family (Mobility)

We do not know when or why Barnabas migrated to Jerusalem. William Cave believes that Barnabas' parents were pious Jews and ". . . they sent or brought him to Jerusalem, to be trained up in the knowledge of the law, and to that end committed him to the tutorage of Gamaliel, the great doctor of the law, and most famous master at that time in Israel . . ." (1840:91). J. A. Robertson also suggests that he was a dedicated Levite who studied in Jerusalem and then became a ruler of the synagogue there (1920:46).

While the new church in Jerusalem was struggling to develop, it is likely that Barnabas had become a part. G. Buchanan Ryley puts forth the theory that Barnabas was already one of the leaders and teachers of the fledgling church. This is based on the fact that Barnabas' name was not in the list of seven people chosen to be deacons (Acts 6:1-7).

> If he was in Jerusalem at the time, it is almost singular, and nearly warrants the supposition that he was counted among the apostolic men who were to continue steadfastly in prayer and in the ministry of the word. . . . The inclusion of Barnabas in such a supposition would go with the meaning of his Christian name, and would additionally support the assured belief of the high esteem in which the Church of Jerusalem held the Son of Exhortation (Ryley 1893:56).

The fact that not long after this Barnabas came on the scene to introduce Paul to the Jerusalem Council, and that his credibility made this possible, makes it seem logical that Barnabas was one of these leaders rather than a rank-and-file member.

Process Item IV: Family (Relatives/Network)

It may have been through relatives that Barnabas met Jesus or at least came into contact with the Jerusalem church, since Mary (whose house was a gathering place for believers) was Barnabas' aunt (Col. 4:10). Also, relatives that may have remained in Cyprus could have smoothed the way for Barnabas when he returned to Cyprus. Finally, we know that Barnabas mentored his cousin John Mark in the final episodes of our biblical account of him. Thus, the network of his relatives played a crucial role in his life.

Table of Principles - Phase I

NAME	OBSERVATION	PRINCIPLES (COMMENTS)
1. Sovereign Background	Barnabas was raised on Cyprus (island worldview) among Greeks (bi-cultural). He was a Levite (religious) and had relatives in Jerusalem (network). His family was mobile.	a. Early details in a life often have long term significance on major selection decisions. (Who was chosen to go to Antioch where Cyprus missionaries had won Greeks to the Lord? A religious Jew who was in Jerusalem, who understood the Cyprus missionaries, and who knew Greeks. This was a major leadership selection decision in Barnabas' life.)

Overview and Detailed Phase Chart:
Phase II (Divine Linking: Maturing in Giftedness)

Important Categories	A. Personal Growth		B. Linking Ministry - Jerusalem		C. Linking Minisry -Antioch		
			1. Jerusalem		2. Paul to Antioch		3. Antioch to Jerusalem
Time Span	←——— 1-2 Years ———→		←——— 1-7 Years ———→		←——— 1-2 Years ———→		
Biblical Data	Acts 4:32-37		Acts 9:23-30 Gal 1:15-19		Acts 11:19-24	Acts 11:25-26	Acts 11:27-30 Gal 2:1-10
Essential Geography	Jerusalem		Jerusalem		Antioch	Antioch Tarsus	Antioch Jerusalem
	←——— First Persecution of Church: scattering ———→						
Context/ Event/ People	Formation of Early Church/ modeling of Apostles	Persecution of Church in Jerusalem	Paul's Conversion	Cornelius' conversion	Gentile conversions in Antioch (missionaries from Cyprus, Cyrene)		Agabus Famine in Jerusalem Herod's Persecution
Major Process Factors/ Detailed Items	**Inner-Life** • Obedience • Giving **Ministry** • Name • Giftedness • Discipline (Ananias & Sapphira)		**Guidance** • Divine contact for Paul/linking		**Guidance** • Sovereign choice • Confermation by apostles **Ministry** • Ministry task (apostolic responsibility) • Spiritual Authority (good man) **Inner-Life** •Word test (Cornelius model used)	**Guidence** • Divine contact (Linking Paul) • Mentoring **Ministry** • Giftedness • Spiritual authority power base; self-initiative; sees need	**Inner-life Growth** • Obedience/ giving word Check **Ministry** • Apostolic bridging • Imitation modeling • Self-initiative
Possible Gift-mix	• Giving • Exhortation • Helps				• Apostleship • Evangelism • Teaching	• Apostleship • Evangelism •Teaching	• Apostleship • Evangelism • Mercy • Giving
Sphere of Influence	Fellow-believers in local Jerusalem church				Local church	Local church	Inter-local church

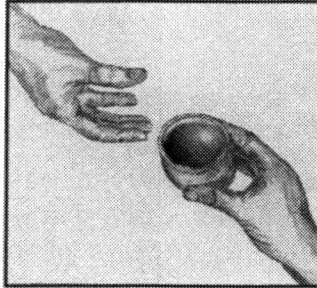

NARRATIVE EXPLANATION OF PHASE II:
DIVINE LINKING;
MATURING IN GIFTEDNESS

Overview

The first mention of Barnabas in the Scriptures (Acts 4:36) teems with implications showing growth in his inner-life. This vignette gives us some hints of Barnabas' early background and responses to Christian truth. Barnabas:

1. was a Jewish Levite from Cyprus (and the Cyprus connection will later be seen to be sovereignly used by God in a major linking function);
2. was a part of the Christian movement while it was vital (growing both in quality and quantity);
3. was early challenged by Christian truth and responded positively to it in sacrificial obedience;
4. early learned the freedom of giving and was able all through life to pass on this essential Christian characteristic;
5. exercised his gift of exhortation in such a way as to encourage others both by his life and words;
6. was recognized by the Jewish leaders as leadership potential;
7. received a name which prophetically set the bent of his life; it was also an expression of Goodwin's expectation principle.

Sub-Phase A: Personal Growth

The major process items in this sub-phase include:
1. Obedience
2. Name expectation
3. Giftedness

Process Item I: Obedience

Barnabas was a person of integrity and was also sensitive to the Holy Spirit. This is revealed in Barnabas' early giving example is contrasted with Ananias and Sapphira. This early observation of Barnabas as a person of potential sets the stage for observing the realization of potential.

Acts 4:32 records that the disciples were "one in heart and mind" in this action, and since Barnabas was one of this group, it indicates that he gave joyfully and responded in obedience to God. Having proved his faithfulness, Barnabas would later be entrusted with greater responsibility by the Holy Spirit.

It might seem strange that a Levite owned land, due to the structure in Numbers 18:30 and the subsequent division of land in Numbers 34, ". . . but the case of Jeremiah (Jer. 33:7-15) shows that the rule was not always strictly observed, for a Levite could buy or inherit a piece of land" (Robertson 1922:32).

Process Item II: Name Expectation

Joseph is referred to as Barnabas for the first time in this passage, and the scripture indicates that the name means Son of Encouragement. Filson says, "No derivation of the Aramaic word 'Barnabas' has been proposed which completely explains the Greek translation given by Luke, 'Son of exhortation'" (1940:84), but Furneaux states, "The Greek word denotes exhortation, consolation, encouragement – all three. There is no English equivalent which covers the same grounds, so that the translator must employ different words according to the context. But since the Hebrew word 'nabas' denotes exhortation, that is certainly the meaning here" (1912:68).

According to the Greek,[10] Barnabas means "Son of Prophecy" (Strong 1890:Greek 921). Cave explains the Greek meaning of this, in accordance with Luke's interpretation (Son of Encouragement), ". . . implying him a 'son of prophecy,' eminent for his prophetic gifts and endowments, or denoting him (what was a peculiar part of the prophets' office) 'a son of consolation,' for his admirable dexterity in erecting troubled minds, and leading them on by the most mild and gentle methods of persuasion: . . ." (Cave 1940:90-91).

---

10. This word is studied in detail in conjunction with the spiritual gift of exhortation. See Appendix A-2 dealing with the definition of the gift of exhortation.

Whatever the meaning, it is obvious that the apostles called him Barnabas because he was an encourager. However, by being given that name, it is likely that he would try even harder to live up to the expectations[11] if the apostles who had conferred this on him.

Process Item III: Giftedness

From this passage, it seems fairly obvious that Barnabas had the spiritual gifts of giving and exhortation and that God was giving him the opportunity to develop them.

In relationship to the gift of giving, it is likely that Barnabas learned to give in the context of the group and under the tutelage of Peter and John who had learned directly from the teachings of Jesus. Barnabas was then able to pass this on to those he discipled (11:29). Also, he probably saw how the selfless giving of the Jerusalem believers allowed the apostles to continue testifying to the resurrection of Christ without being diverted by financial matter.

The passage also shows that "If nothing else, he showed that he was not only an exhorter, a consoler by word, a speech-maker but also a willing sacrifice for Christ" (Ryley 1893:35). Ryley goes on to say:

> His act must have been, in some way, prominent in the self-stripping and full consecration of the Church members. Else, why name him at all? Or, why put him and his deed in awful contrast with the living lie to the Holy Ghost of Ananias and Sapphira? . . . . As Abraham was to Lot and his wife, so was Barnabas to Ananias and Sapphira (1893:36).

Sub-Phase B: Linking Ministry – Jerusalem

The only process item in this sub-phase is:
1. Divine contact for Paul/linking

Process Item I: Divine Contact for Paul/Linking

Paul had spent time with the disciples in Damascus (9:19), but when he came to Jerusalem and trued to break into the "in" group (the power base of Christianity), the disciples were afraid of him. "The imperfect tense again shows that Saul did not give up without a struggle" (Robertson 1922:34). After how Paul had persecuted the Christians, the disciples were afraid in case his purported conversion was only a trick.

> It may seem strange that the conversion of Saul was at most only a rumour in Jerusalem after the space of some three years. But Saul spent most of that time in Arabia, and his own conduct as

---

11. This illustrates Goodwin's Expectation Principle (footnote 6).

the leader of the Pharisaic persecution in Jerusalem was enough to throw suspicion upon any reports of his change of heart and life in Damascus. Besides, the Sanhedrin may have spread sinister rumours about Saul's probable motives in his avowal of Christianity. His prolonged absence from Jerusalem was in itself peculiar, and he brought no letters of recommendation from the Christians in Damascus (Robertson 1922:34).

It is at this critical point that Barnabas stepped in and began his linking ministry. He saw the potential in Paul and took him to Peter and James which provided the opportunity for him to become credible to the Christian community. Barnabas had taken the trouble to find out Paul's testimony and how he had preached fearlessly at Damascus, was willing to believe Paul's story and then spoke on his behalf to the apostles, risking his own credibility with the apostles. We are not told if Barnabas had assessed Paul's word for this or if he had outside confirmation, but in either case, he risked his reputation for the sake of introducing Paul.

It is also important to note that by this time Barnabas had acquired sufficient influence with the apostles that his speaking in behalf of Paul was enough for Paul to be accepted. He was respected for his life, ministry and judgment, a sign of spiritual authority. This divine contact with Paul was to be the key to God's expansion of Christianity to a Gentile world. ". . . Paul himself reveals in Gal. 2:1ff. how important that connection was to him and how radically it conditioned the success of his work" (Filson 1940:103).

It is, of course, inconceivable that Saul would have forsaken the work of the Lord if the apostles and Jerusalem Church had passed him by; for he was Christ's 'chosen vessel.' But it is at least supposable that, if Saul had been once driven from Jerusalem in the early days of his Christian faith, by the fear, coldness and suspicion of the Church and apostles, as well as by the hate of his Hebrew enemies, his heart and faith would have been strained by a trial that would have marked all his after history, even though he had mastered the disappointment and sadness of such an experience (Ryley 1893:66).

Barnabas avoided this by being God's divine contact and linker for Paul.

Sub-Phase C: Linking Ministry – Antioch

The most important process items in sub-phase C are:
1. Confirmation by apostles
2. Ministry task (apostolic responsibility)
3. Spiritual authority in two incidents (good man; self-initiative)
4. Divine contact (linking for Paul)
5. Imitation modeling

Process Item I: Confirmation by Apostles

When the church in Jerusalem heard that the Gospel was being preached to Greeks in Antioch, the apostles confirmed the leading of the Holy Spirit in choosing Barnabas to investigate the matter. "It is proof of the high position of Barnabas in the Jerusalem Church that he was chosen (Acts 11:22) as a committee of one (cf. Acts 8:14) to investigate conditions in Antioch, . . . "(Robertson 1922:37-38). When there had been previous incidents in Samaria, Peter and John had gone. So, that Barnabas was sent on this task indicates that he had risen greatly in prestige. Otherwise he would not have been entrusted with this apostolic task of testing the genuineness of this Christian expression.

What were the "human" factors for the apostles choosing Barnabas? First, he was "a good man, full of the Holy Spirit and faith, . . ." (Acts 11:24), traits that gave him influence and leadership (Jacobs 1957:405). Comments such as this one made about Barnabas are ". . . very rare in the New Testament, and ought to carry the greater meaning, wherever they occur, because of their rarity" (Ryley 1893:92). He must have had "a profound humility, diffusive charity, firm faith, an immovable constancy, and an unconquerable patience, a mighty zeal, and an unwearied diligence in the propagating of Christianity, and for the good of souls. . ." (Cave 1840:102).

Secondly, some of those who had come to Antioch and were sharing with the Greeks were from Cyprus, Barnabas' home, and so he would more likely understand them and their worldview. Here we see Barnabas' sovereign foundations coming into play.

Thirdly, the apostles trusted him to check out the genuineness of this new innovation in light of his Jewish heritage as well as his previous exposure to the Roman world and the Jews of the Dispersion on the island of Cyprus. The Jerusalem church had just experienced through Peter a practical test of Jesus' command to share the Gospel throughout the world. This was through Peter's vision and interaction with Cornelius. The apostles in Jerusalem had heard about this and criticized Peter, but when he explained, they had no further objections and acknowledged, "So then, God has even granted the Gentiles repentance unto life" (Acts 11:8). Now it was not just one Gentile who had become a believer but the beginning of a movement.

As a Levite, the apostles trusted that Barnabas knew and valued his Jewish heritage (Filson 1940:99). But also,

> It is exceedingly important for us to observe that in reaching the first Gentiles who were brought into the Christian Church, the Spirit of God did not use men utterly unacquainted with Gentile life. The progress of the gospel depended then as now upon prepared men. Only through members of the Jewish race who already possessed considerable understanding of Gentile people and needs could the gospel be carried out into the Roman world. The presentation of the gospel had to be made by men who had real points of contact with the life of the people to whom they went (Filson 1940:96-97).

Barnabas may have been selected also because his

> . . . Hellenistic origin would commend him to the Christians at Antioch, and so enable him to carry out the difficult task of persuading the new converts to accept the views of Jerusalem without raising the delicate question of the right of that part of the church to express any opinion in the matter at all. The fact that he appeared alone and not in the company of a colleague of Apostolic rank would tend to divest his visit of the appearance of a formal Apostolic visitation to settle the affairs of the Church of Antioch. Since Peter and his colleagues had not been consulted on the matter, it was obviously desirable to avoid any such appearance (Knox 1925:158).

Another reason why Barnabas was chosen could well have been his spiritual gifts, which at this point probably included apostleship, exhortation and evangelism which were precisely what was needed for this situation. "Barnabas was a son of exhortation, consolation, and encouragement to these Greek Christians" (Robertson 1922:40). A great number were brought to the Lord (Acts 11:24) which reveals his gift of evangelism.

While not a spiritual gift, Barnabas had probably already exhibited a talent for mentoring, which meant he had the ability to act as a bridge between two different parties or points of view. Filson mentions the "Other men may do more spectacular work. None, however, will ever do a more important work than is done by such men as Barnabas, who command the respect of opposite sides when misunderstanding arises or difference is acute" (1940:101).

Process Item II: Ministry Task (Apostolic Responsibility)

The Jewish Christian leaders through the providence of God appointed Barnabas to investigate the Antioch manifestation of Christianity. Barnabas' sovereign foundations (his island worldview, familiarity with Greeks, Cyprus connections), his positive growth in ministry and spiritual authority, and his experiential understanding of Christianity (Cornelius' revelation) were used by God to select Barnabas for this apostolic ministry task.

Barnabas was responsible for determining if the variations in the Antioch community of believers (acceptance of Gentiles) was a valid form of the new faith. Having seen "the evidence of the grace of God," Barnabas was glad and encouraged them to continue true to the Lord. This implies that "He accepted the Greek Christians as fully on a par with the Jewish Christians. The whole Church lined free from the Jewish ceremonial restrictions (Acts 15:1; Gal. 2:11-14)" (Robertson 1922:40). He was able to rise above his Jewish traditions and prejudices by seeing

> . . . that God had broken down the middle wall of partition and had saved these Greeks without their becoming Jews. . . He re-adjusted his theology, if necessary, to suit the evident work of God, . . . He had convictions, but he was able to see facts that contravened them and to accept them openly and frankly (Robertson 1922:39).

As part of his mentoring qualities, Barnabas was glad (Acts 11:23) over what he discovered in Antioch and rejoiced in the others' enthusiasm for ministry. While there may have been problems and excesses, he saw it as an opportunity in which the problems could be corrected over a period of time. It would be in this process that his gift of exhortation would play a vital role. Barnabas' attitude toward this new movement was an integrity check from God in his own inner growth, for he could well have condemned the innovations made in contextualizing the gospel.

Barnabas was so interested in helping develop this group of Christians with their innovations in the application of the Gospel message that he stayed to help guide the church. "It is a tribute to his [Barnabas'] worth and ability that although he had not helped to found the church, all accepted his leadership" (Filson 1940:99).

Barnabas did well in this first apostolic ministry test. He was able to judge the manifestations he saw in light if the word of truth he knew and give a positive recommendation that this was genuine Christianity. His gifts of apostleship and exhortation were in focus during this visit. He was able to link this Gentile Christianity with the Jewish Christianity at Jerusalem, and he built a sound base of relationships at Antioch from which he could correct problems he saw with the Gentile Christianity.

Process Item III: Spiritual Authority

In two separate incidents within this phase, evidence is shown of Barnabas' spiritual authority. Acts 11:24 mentions he was "a good man, full of the Holy Spirit and faith." His life before the community of faith gave great credibility in their eyes.

Soon after Barnabas arrived in Antioch, he went to Tarsus to find Paul. This shows that Barnabas saw a need and used his own initiative to help solve it, which is an indication of apostolic ministry. But it also shows that he had enough credibility (spiritual authority) to bring this new, previously hated, person into the midst of the believers and have him be accepted.

Process Item IV: Divine Contact (Linking for Paul)

We do not know why Barnabas went to Tarsus to find Paul, nor do we know what Paul had been doing in the three years since his conversion. However,

> Of one thing we are certain: he had been preaching the Gospel (Gal. 1:23). This work was done, mainly at least, in his native Cilicia (Acts 9:30), although the mention of "Syria and Cilicia" in Gal. 1:21 may be taken to mean that on the way to Cilicia Paul preached for a brief time in Syria. We do not know either how widely this preaching had extended or how successful it was. Probably we are justified in concluding, from the fact that Barnabas sought him out for a place of leadership at Antioch, and from the mention of churches in Cilicia in Acts 15:41, that his work in Cilicia had been successful and that word of his fruitful activity had reached Antioch (Filson 1940:103-104).

Robertson (1922:40) and Cave (1840:93) feel that Barnabas decided there was too much work for him at Antioch, but in light of the others who had come to Antioch before him and were still there (Acts 13:1), this does not seem a likely reason. It is more probable that Barnabas recognized the potential in Paul and sought him out to give him opportunities to grow, especially since the Antioch church was dynamic and now "sanctioned" by the Jerusalem church. This co-ministry with Paul did three major things. It brought Paul into the mainstream of Christianity, it helped him develop his ministry gifts and status, and it built up the Antioch church. This is evidenced by the term "Christians" first being used at Antioch and later by the mention of Paul as being one of the teachers.

Barnabas brought Paul into the mainstream of Christianity. Paul's background would make him open to understanding the inclusion of the Gentiles in the church at Antioch and the church would benefit from his ministry. Once again Barnabas functioned in a linking role and through this incident moved from being only a divine contact in Paul's life to being his mentor.

Barnabas' love of giving influenced the Antioch church. When Agabus gave a word of prophet regarding the famine, their response indicated the reality of the doctrine of giving in their life-styles. In addition to linking two churches at the regional level (Antioch and Judea) more firmly together, this task of taking the offering to Jerusalem would further help Paul be accepted by the Jewish Christians outside his previous areas of ministry. It would also help them recognize Paul's experiential growth in ministry tendencies. And God rewarded Barnabas' positive response by outward conformation of a sense of destiny. Barnabas and Paul were recognized by the Jewish Christian leaders as apostles to the Gentiles.

Process Item V: Imitation Modeling

Together Barnabas and Paul taught. Here again Barnabas played a mentoring role wherein he took the lead but also provided opportunities for Paul to learn and grow over the period of a year. This in itself was an act and process of encouraging. From Acts 13:1 we can infer that Barnabas was the foremost teacher at Antioch, while Paul was at the bottom of the list of teachers and prophets in influence. Since Barnabas and Paul are the only two mentioned in 12:26, it can be assumed that Paul was teaching with and under Barnabas. It was Barnabas' credibility which established Paul in his teaching. Whether it was due to the success of Barnabas and Paul's efforts (and the lives they lived before the community), or due to other factors, the believers at Antioch lived such an exemplary life as to be the first to be called Christians (Christ-ones, who reflect the image of Christ).

Barnabas also greatly affected the believers at Antioch by his modeling of giving to the Lord. His exhortations were based on his own personal learning about giving (4:36). He had previously modeled his giving; now he encouraged others toward it, so Paul (and others) had a chance to experientially learn. The church at Antioch (i.e. "each according to his ability") responded to the word of the Lord through the prophet Agabus and collected money to offset the famine in Judea. Later Paul would write about this (Phil. 4, II Cor. 8,9).

Table of Principles - Phase II

Name	Observation	Principles (Comments)
1. Exhortation Base	Barnabas early experienced life changing application of Christianity in the context of modeling and community (obedience to request to share, etc.) which he passed on to others.	a. One who exhorts does so best out of personal life-changing experiences (Barnabas: giving - Antioch church gives - Paul giving).
2. Early Lessons	Barnabas responded to teaching concerning sacrifical giving.	a. Leaders are often tested early-on with regards to obedience and finances. Response to these will lead to expanded personal growth and ministry.
3. Goodwin's Expectation Principle	The apostles in Jerusalem recognized potential in Barnabas (his exhortation gift was singled out). They saw his ministry of encouragement and his response to God.	a. A follower tends to live up to live up to genuine expectations of leader(s) he/she respects.
4. Giftedness	The apostles gave outside confirmation of Barnabas's gifts. Name change. Barnabas greatly encouraged.	a. Name changes often signify bent of life characteristics (Son of Encouragement). b. One with the gift of exhortation should recognize the powerful influence of encouragement. c. One with the gift of exhortation can use a personal life-changing application of Christianity to impact and encourage others.
5. Divine Discipline	Barnabas observed the Ananias and Sapphira discipline.	a. Honesty and integrity are qualities very important to God - God sometimes go to unusual lengths to stress this to an emerging leader.
6. Divine Contact	God impressed upon Barnabas the need to accept and trust Paul and recommend him to the apostles. This proved to be divine contact. Barnabas was there at an opportune time moment for Paul.	a. God often brings "significant persons" across our lives at very opportune moments to perform some necessary "guidance function." (Often the divine contacts will reappear later on in life and influence us again).

Table of Principles - Phase II Cont.

Name	Observation	Principles (Comments)
7. Sovereign Choice	Barnabas was God's man for God's task. His family background, exhortation gift and what he had learned through divine experiences had uniquely prepared for the tasks ahead.	a. Through family background, spiritual gifts and experiences, God prepares leaders for unknown tasks ahead.
8. Confirmation by Apostles	It was the church in Jerusalem, headed by the apostles, which recognized that Barnabas was the right person to send to Antioch	a. Spiritual leaders need to be sensitive to God's preparation in the lives of emerging leaders. b. Leaders need to respond to God's leading by entrusting responsibility to those God has selected for a task.
9. Ministry Task (Apostolic Functions)	Barnabas was given a ministry task by the Jerusalem apostles(with sovereign foundations definately involved in the decision). The task was a testing of Barnabas' aposolic giftedness, for it involved evaluation of ministry.	a. Apostolic function - test genuineness of Christian expression. b. Apostolic function - must be able to apply word to new situations. c. Apostolic function - build a base of relationships majoring on opportunities rather than problems (then after the base is built, deal with problems). d. Apostolic function - imitation modeling - basic lessons of Christianity best learned in community through example (experiential learning - good man - full of the Holy Spirit - at Antioch called Christians). e. Apostolic function - Build relationships between the wider body (Jew and Gentile). f. Ministry task may be assigned to others to show who show potental. g. Maturity in gift-mix. Exhortation strong. Seen in application to lives and teaching. Learned knowledge, effect (Christ ones), mercy. Gave apostolic truth. Got entire church to respond to Word. Developed the church substantially.
10. Spiritual Authority	Barnabas was recognized as a good man full of the Holy Spirit.	a. An outsider coming into a community needs to show evidence of spiritual authority through his/her life and ministry before a full ministry can be developed. b. Members of a spiritual community need to recognize the spiritual authority of the leaders and emerging leaders.
11. Application of Biblical Truth	Cornelius, a Gentile, recieved a vision to summon Peter. Peter came to realize that God accepts people from all nations	a. After learning of a truth God has revealed to others, a test often occurs in a leader's life wherin the person needs to apply the theory in a practical situation.

Table of Principles-Phase II cont.

Name	Observation	Principles (Comments)
12. Mentoring	Barnabas acted as mentor (sponsor) for Paul both in Jerusalem and Antioch. He displayed mentor qualities throughout their relationship.	a. A mentor has the insight to see potential in a leader although the person may have a bad reputation or abrasive personality traits. (Often strong leadership qualities are hidden beneath confrontative, abrasive, impatient personalities). b. A mentor is willing to take a risk and sponsor a potential leader. c. A mentor focuses on the good qualities and tries to to develop them. d. A mentor is willing to co-minister with a potential leader in order to raise the experience and status of the leader. e. A mentor essentially bridges the potential leader to needed development (networking). f. The mentoree learns through imitation modeling, so the mentor needs to provide a good model.
13. Giftedness Tested	Barnabas sought out and brought him to Antioch. Together they taught in the church.	a. Someone with the gift of encouragement comes alongside a potential leader and rejoices in the developing ministry. The leader does not kill the potential leader's enthusiam.
14. Spiritual Authority	Barnabas brought Paul to Antioch and they taught great numbers.	a. A spiritual leader will see the need and take the initiative to meet the need. b. More can usually be accomplished where a power base has already been established.
15. Self-Initiative	Barnabas saw a need at Antioch. He also knew that the situation would be good for developing Paul's ministry gifts. Therefore, he took initiative to get Paul and used his spiritual authority to get him accepted.	a. An emerging leaders takes the initiative to instigate ministry and solve problems (Self-initiated ministry is one of the outward signs of an emerging leader.) b. God wants us to willingly reaspond to promptings and many times does not want us to wait for direct orders.
16. Word Check (Obedience/Giving)	Agabus predicted a famine and the church in Antioch responded even before the famine occurred.	a. The community of believers needs to respond on faith, not by sight. b. When there is a need, each believer should give according to his/her ability.
17. Bridging	In response to Agabus' prediction of famine, the church at Antioch sent a contribution with Barnabas and Paul to Jerusalem to help the churches in Judea.	a. Giving can be a means of linking with the larger Christian community. b. Great responsibility needs to be entrusted to faithful servants.
18. Imitation Modeling	Barnabas had previously learned giving (acts 4:36-37), so it is likely that he set the example for the church at Antoich in giving.	a. What we have learned from God we need to demonstrate in our lives for others to follow. b. A leader can have a powerful impact through his/her example.

Overview and Detailed Phase Chart:
Phase III (Apostolic convergence among Gentiles)

Important Categories	A. Team Leadership		B. Leadership Transition		C. Emerging Gentile Church Definition	
	1. Antioch	2. Cyprus	1. Transition	2. Leadership Transition	3. Continued Conflict	
Time Span	1-2 Months			9 Months		
Biblical Data	Acts 13:1-3	Acts 13:4-12	Acts 13:13-52	Acts 14:1-7	Acts 14:8-20	Acts 14:21-25
Essential Geography	Antioch	Cyprus	Perga Antioch (Pisidia)	Iconium	Lystra/ Derbe (Lycaonia)	Iconium et al.
Context/ Events/ People	Simeon Lucius Manaen 2nd persecution in Jerusalem	John Mark Sergius Paulus Bar-Jesus (Elymans)	John Mark Jewish Backlash			
Major Process Factors/ Detailed Items	**Maturity** • Sense of Destiny (call of H.S.) **Guidance** • Soverign Guidance (prophetic confirmation)	**Ministry** • Power encounter • Name contextualization for Paul **Guidance** • Mentoring (John Mark)	**Ministry** • Conflict (John Mark) • Authority switch (submission by Barnabas) • Cross-Cultural Strategy • Conversions • Success • Backlash	**Ministry** • Leadership backlash • Success **Guidance** • Divine confirmation	**Ministry** • Conflict • Power encounter • Word factor • Contextualization • Giftedness • Persecution	**Ministry** • Giftedness • Success • Apostolic function (church leaders appointed)
Possible Gift-Mix	• Apostleship	• Apostleship • Miracles	• Apostleship • Exhortation • Evangelism	• Apostleship • Evangelism • Miracles	• Apostleship • Healing • Word of Knowledge	• Apostleship • Evangelism • Exhortation
Sphere of Influence	Metropolitan local church (level 3 leaders)	Bi-national	Multi-national	Multi-national	Multi-national church/fellowships	Multi-national churches

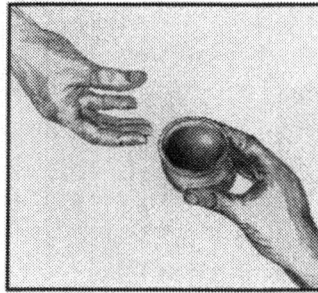

NARRATIVE EXPLANATION OF PHASE III:
APOSTOLIC CONVERGENCE AMONG GENTILES

Overview

Barnabas worked in the Antioch church for about a year where he evidenced the mature use of the spiritual gifts of apostleship, teaching and exhortation, and possibly mercy and giving were also a part of his gift-mix. Although multi-gifted, his dominant gift was exhortation. His spiritual authority was sound and attested to by the Jewish Christians leaders and the Antioch church in general.

Within the Antioch church were a number of Gentile believers, and it was from this base that Barnabas and Paul branched out into other areas of the Gentile world to share the gospel message. Barnabas and Paul were released by the church and sent forth by the Holy Spirit for this second crucial ministry task – setting the pattern of expansion of Christianity among the Gentiles. Barnabas, true to his exhortive gift and mentoring experience took along a protege, John Mark who would develop in an informal apprenticeship. Initially they went to Jewish synagogues, and only when the Jews refused to listen did they turn to the Gentiles. Later they realized it would be necessary for the believing communities to be separate from the synagogues and appointed elders over these groups. Thus, the Gentile church emerged.

Sub-Phase A: Team Leadership

The important process items in this phase are:
1. Sense of destiny
2. Power encounter
3. Name contextualization

Process Item I: Sense of Destiny

The Holy Spirit telling the church to set apart Barnabas and Paul for the work to which they were called must have been a real sense of destiny experience for both of Barnabas and Paul. "Saul's life and ministry among the believers in Antioch must have largely qualified him for the mission work among the Gentiles, to which, with Barnabas, he was ordained by the Church" (Ryley 1893:98). However, Paul was not quite ready to launch out on his own, and thus the Holy Spirit directed both of them on the journey. So Barnabas continued in his mentoring role.

It is important to note that the position Barnabas gave up in the church for this journey was one of eminence, thus indicating his humility and sense of servant leadership. He was not too entrenched in a position to move on to work God had before him.

Process Item II: Power Encounter

It was at Paphos where Barnabas and Paul encountered Elymas the sorcerer, which lead to a power encounter.[12] Cyprus was a natural location for the first experience in cross-cultural evangelism due to Barnabas' connections. Fundamental lessons on power and the need to contextualize the Jewish message were first learned here. Elymas opposed the gospel and trued to turn the proconsul away from the faith. This had clearly become a spiritual battle. Paul then challenged him and prophesied that Elymas would become blind for a period of time. By fulfilling this prophesy, God showed that he had truly empowered the ministry of Barnabas and Paul. Upon seeing this, the proconsul believed. It must also have given Barnabas and Paul much greater confidence in the ministry they had.

Process Phase III: Name Contextualization

It was at this point that Saul's name was contextualized for the Gentile world, and he was thereafter called Paul.

Sub-Phase B: Leadership Transition

This sub-phase is principally characterized by the following process items:
1. Authority switch
2. Success
3. Backlash
4. Contextualization
5. Giftedness

---

12. "Power encounter" is a word made popular in the writings of A. R. Tippett, one of the early missiologists of the School of World Mission, Fuller Theological Seminary. See Chapter 7, "Problems of Encounter," in his book *Solomon Island Christianity* which defines and illustrates power encounters.

Process Item I: Authority Switch

Barnabas had co-ministered with Paul for some time, and Paul's leadership potential had reached the point where it needed to be released. Exactly how this came about is not recorded. Acts 13:9 is the first time Scripture indicates Paul taking the lead. Perhaps by coming into a new environment Paul was no longer "under the shadow of Barnabas' great reputation in Antioch" (Robertson 1922:43-44), and so it was then possible for him to come to the forefront.

> Barnabas served Christ incomparably by taking a second place.
> . . . Very few would discover a prime condition of the growth of the Church, and the progress of the truth as it is in Jesus, in their own voluntary effort to bring forward another man, who could more effectively meet the need of the time and place" (Ryley 1893:103).

But Barnabas "was quick to see the larger opportunity for the spread of the faith and allow Paul to take the place of prominence" (Filson 1940:100).

That the authority switch came about is clearly indicated in the phrase, "Paul and his companions sailed from Paphos and came to Perga." By Acts 13:13 Paul had taken so much of the lead/authority that Barnabas is not even mentioned by name, and from 14:42 when both are mentioned, Paul is usually in the foremost position. The exceptions can easily be explained in the particular situations.

While it is not mentioned why John Mark chose to leave the group, considering that Barnabas, an encourager and John Mark's cousin, lead the group at the beginning of the journey. it is likely that John Mark was not happy with Paul's emerging leadership. This is in stark contrast to Barnabas' maturity in allowing another person to take the lead over him. One of the great expressions of a mentor is seen in Barnabas' reaction to this authority switch. By this time, Barnabas had almost completed his mentoring role with Paul.

Process Item II: Success

Throughout their journey and this phase of Barnabas' life, Paul and Barnabas had a positive response to the gospel they shared. In the process they must have grown in their own faith, learned more about sharing the gospel message with non-believers (and especially with non-Jews) and been impressed with how God continued to evidence his presence with them.

Process Item III: Backlash

During this phase, success is mentioned in Acts 13:42-44, 13:48-49, 14:1, 14:3 and 14:18 (although this episode does not mention conversions but only a response to Paul and Barnabas). Correspondingly, in Acts 13:45, 13:50, 14:2, 14:5 and 14:19 there were repercussions to their ministry. While these were probably difficult times for the two men, it showed that they were making and impact on the populace. It also had the important side effect of making them turn to preach the gospel to the Gentiles since the Jews rejected it.

Process Item IV: Contextualization

It was the healing of the crippled man and the subsequent identification of Paul and Barnabas with Hermes and Zeus that allowed them to share their message in contextualized terms. They spoke of turning from objects to a living God who left his testimony through nature. However, the people did not respond in the desired way and instead were turned against Paul and Barnabas by some Jews from Antioch Pisidia. So the team moved on again.

Together Barnabas and Paul learned about contextualization of the Gospel, the need for power confirmation of the message in new cultures, the need under conflict and pressure to separate believers into autonomous structures, and the need to establish and release leaders to grow into ministry and spiritual authority. This pattern was to become the dominant pattern for cross-cultural ministry by Paul in the rest of his missionary career.

Process Item V: Giftedness

Throughout this phase we see Barnabas and Paul's spiritual gifts coming into play. First, in Acts 13:15, we see the synagogue rulers asking them for a word of encouragement.

In Lystra, a crippled man heard Paul's preaching. Paul apparently received a word of knowledge about this, for it records that Paul "saw that he had faith to be healed." Their ministry was then validated by the gift of healing. There had also been miraculous signs in Iconium (14:3).

The gift of evangelism is evidenced in 13:49 and 14:1.

Although Barnabas is previously referred to as a prophet and teacher, it is in 14:14 that he is mentioned as an apostle for the first time. In the early years of the church a wider meaning of the term "apostle" than just referring to the Twelve was current. "Paul is sometimes held responsible for this. Certainly, he uses the work in a wider sense, and speaks not only of himself but also of Barnabas (I Cor. 9:6) and others (Rom. 16:7) as apostles" (Filson 1940:165).

Sub-Phase C: Emerging Gentile Church Definition

The predominant process items in this sub-phase are:
1. Giftedness
2. Apostolic function (church leaders appointed)

Process Item I: Giftedness

Returning to Lystra, Iconium and Antioch Pisidia, Paul and Barnabas encouraged the disciples to remain true to the faith. In talking of hardships, it hardly seems like what modern Americans think of as encouragement. However, true encouragement gives the recipient the courage and strength to endure whatever is necessary to achieve the goal.

Process Item II: Apostolic Function (Church Leaders Appointed)

By this time it appears that local churches had begun to separate from the synagogues, and Paul and Barnabas provided the apostolic function of appointing elders in each church. By waiting until this time, individuals within the group of believers had had the opportunity to use their spiritual gifts and to demonstrate spiritual leadership.

Table of Principles - Phase III

Name	Observation	Principles (Comments)
1. Sense of Destiny	The Holy Spirit instructed the church at Antioch to set aside Barnabas and Paul for the Work to which they were called.	a. God will often give a person a sense of destiny to carry the person through with a vision and a goal for life.
2. Prophetic Confirmation	The church at Antioch fasted and pray before responding to the message of the Holy Spirit and sending Barnabas and Paul on their journey.	a. The community of believers needs to commune with God before taking action. b. Fasting can give special awareness to the will of God.
3. Power Encounter	Elymas the Sorcerer opposed Barnabas and Paul and tried to turn the proconsul from faith. Paul predicted that the hand of the Lord was against him and he would be blind for a time. This came to pass.	a. God will demonstrate his power to establish his truth and convince people that he is with the leader in the ministry. b. There must be recognition that the issue is one of confrontation in the spiritual realm. c. God at times displays a sense of irony. Elymas was blind to the spiritual truth, so God made him blind in the physical realm as well.
4. Name Contextualization	Saul's name changes to Paul.	a. We need to present ourselves and our message so that our audience can understand.
5. Conflict (John Mark)	John Mark left because Paul took over leadership.	a. We need to be flexible to the changing scene of God. b. We need to place ourselves under the submission of God's person for that time.
6. Authority Switch	When Paul takes over the leadership, Barnabas willingly steps back into a secondary role.	a. In mentoring a developing leader, he/she may surpass the mentor. At this point the mentor must step aside to allow further development. b. At particular times God may choose to have a different leader, and the previous leader needs to be humble and submissive to his will.
7. Cross-Cultural Strategy	Paul and Barnabas gave the Gentiles the message that God had appointed them to be light to the Gentiles and bring salvation to the ends of th earth.	a. To effectively present the gospel cross-culturally, we need to meet a felt need (apparently in this case, salvation).

Table of Principles - Phase III Cont.

Name	Observation	Principles (Comments)
8. Backlash	After a great number of people believed, there was a plot to stone Paul and Barnabas.	a. A successful minitry may bring backlash because of the inherent ramifications of that minstry.
9. Divine Confirmation	At Iconium, after a great many believed, unbelieving Jews poisoned the minds of the brothers. God confirmed Paul and Barnabas' message by enabling them to do miraculous signs and wonders.	a. When inroads of doubt are attacking a new community of believers, God will do what is necessary to establish their faith.
10. Contextualization	After the Lycaonians thought Paul and Barnabas were gods, Paul used the event to preach the gospel, sharing in terms of the living God who leaves a testimony to himself through nature.	a. In sharing the gospel, we need to take advantage of the opportunity with which God presents us. b. To make the gospel meaningful to non-believers, we need to share the message in the context of what the people can understand.
11. Giftedness	Paul and Barnabas used their gifts in good measure: evangelism won a large number of disciples; encouragement strengthened the disciples to remain true to the faith; apostleship allowed them to appoint church leaders.	a. It is important to use all the gifts God has given and at the appropriate times. b. God provides those gifts which are necessary for the ministry to which he calls a person. c. Even after a comunity of believers is established, it often need further encouragement to remain true to the faith. d. Encouragement often is not the soft kind of thing we picture it today; Paul and Barnabas encouraged the people by warning them of the hardships they must undergo to enter the kingdom of God.
12. Apostolic Function (Church Leaders Appointed)	"Paul and Barnabas appointed elders for them in each church and, with prayer and fasting, committed them to the Lord in whom they had put their trust" (Acts 14:23).	a. A community of believers need to be separated unto itself (e.g. they were separated from the synagogue). b. A community of believers need divinely appointed leaders. c. The commissioning of leaders need to be don with leaders need to be done with all seriousness and special communion.

Overview and Detailed Phase Chart:
Phase IV (Further Apostolic Ministry)

Important Categories	A. Reflection	B. Linking		C. Cyprus Church Development
Time Span	One Year			
Biblical Data	Acts 14:26-28	Acts 15:1-35	Gal. 2:11-14	Acts 15:36-41 I Cor. 9:6
Essential Geography	Antioch (Pisidia) Perga Antioch	Jerusalem		Cyprus
Context/Events/ People	•Judaizers to Antioch and South Galatian churches; other daughter churches • Peter	Jerusalem Council		Dispute with Paul
Major Process Factors/ Detailed Items	**Ministry** • Ministry Task (completion report)	**Ministry** • Conflict (Jerusalem Jews); Contextualization (theory and practice) • Conflict (apostolic); confrontation with Peter/Barnabas • Conflict (possible church splits: Antioch with Jerusalem: Antioch with daughter churches in S. Galatia -- Judaizers) • Information distribution (15:3) • Ministry Task (resolution of conflict at highest authority level) • Linker (Barnabas leads in the report, 15:12; obligations called in; he is well known and respected among the Jerusalem leaders) • Linker back -- to Antioch (province)(news/letter/ confirmation); Judas (prophetic exhortation) • Guidance: H.S. consensus (v. 28) • Power inherent in team ministry (gift supported)		**Ministry** • Conflict - with Paul over second trip • Ministry Task - takes Mark • Sphere of influence • Mentoring - John Mark (Col. 4:10, Philemon 23, 2 Tim. 4:11)
Possible Gift-Mix	• Apostleship • Teaching	• Apostleship • Teaching		• Apostleship
Sphere of Influence	Multi-National Churches	Multi-National		National (Cyprus)

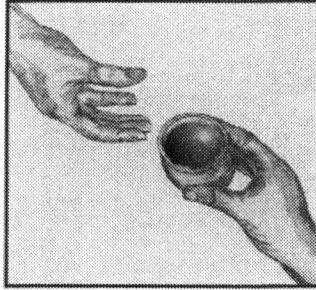

NARRATIVE EXPLANATION OF PHASE IV:
FURTHER APOSTOLIC MINISTRY

Overview

Paul and Barnabas returned to Antioch, their "home base," and shared what God had done. While they were there, the issue of forcing Gentiles to conform to Jewish regulations arose, and they were consequently sent to Jerusalem to settle the matter.

Following the resolution of this issue, Paul wanted to return to churches they had previously planted, but he disagreed with Barnabas' plan to bring John Mark along. Therefore, on this note of conflict Paul and Barnabas split, with Barnabas taking John Mark with him to Cyprus.

Sub-Phase A: Reflection

The process item of this sub-phase is:
1. Ministry task (completion report)

Process Item I: Ministry Task (Completion Report)

While sailing back to their home base of Antioch, Paul and Barnabas had a chance to dynamically reflect on the ministry they had had on this journey and knew that they had completed the work that had been committed to them. They not only reported to the church to Antioch what had happened but also instructed the church in what they had been learning through their experiences. They remained with the Antioch church a long time. This again may well have provided time for them to reflect dynamically. It must also have provided them with a sense of closure regarding the missionary journey.

Sub-Phase B: Linking

The major process times of this sub-phase are:
1. Conflict
2. Ministry task (resolution of conflict at highest authority level)
3. Linking

Process Item I: Conflict

Conflict seemed to be an important item in this sub-phase, for the issue at stake was whether the Gentiles had to conform to Jewish standards, and as a result, whether Jews could fellowship with Gentiles. It is likely that Luke received his account in Acts 15 from Barnabas, for Paul's account in Galatians 2 is not quite so conciliatory (Robertson 1920:136).

Up until this time, Barnabas "had established himself as a champion of Gentile Christianity. For some years he had been the leader of the Antioch church, where Jews and Gentiles had come together in a common Christian fellowship unmarred by any sense of separation" (Filson 1940:86). In his missionary adventures, the gospel had been successfully presented to Gentiles. Plus he had defended the non-circumcision of Gentiles before the Jerusalem Council (Gal. 2:1-10). But in spite of the Jerusalem Council agreeing that Gentiles did not have to assume the obligations of the Jewish law, social equality, as indicated by Jewish food regulations (Filson 1940:87), between Jew and Gentile "had not been passed upon by the Jerusalem conference. It was simply assumed here in Antioch" (Robertson 1922:47).

The conflict created from within the church by Jewish Christians with a narrow understanding of Christian truth threatened to split the Antioch Christians from a large number of regional churches. Then representatives came from "faith-by-works" James and taught that the Gentiles must be circumcised. Peter, who had been eating with Gentiles, drew away. Barnabas, as was typical of his bridging experience, sought to help Peter in the conflict. Paul strongly opposed both and convinced them of the seriousness of what they were modeling. "The effect was to split a previously united brotherhood. Paul clearly indicates that this action of Barnabas was most unusual; he says that '*even* Barnabas was carried away by their hypocrisy.' In other words, Barnabas was the last person whom Paul would have expected to yield to this divisive movement" (Filson 1940:87).

Various authors have expounded greatly over Barnabas' slip at this point. But whether it was because he was tied to his Jewish roots, he tried to be a mediating factor between the two groups as was a natural quality in his personality, or he lacked in courage and firmness, the fact that Barnabas did yield "shows that he lacked something of that deep insight into fundamental truth which marked the career of Paul and made him the outstanding apostle to the Gentiles" (Filson 1940:87).

It is quite possible that since the outreach to Gentiles really started at Antioch, Paul felt it was especially important to hold firm here. At any rate, the issue brought Paul and Barnabas into "sharp dispute" (Acts 15:2) with those promoting circumcision. This indicates that Barnabas rapidly realized his error and joined Paul in the debate probably due to his prior ministry to the Gentiles and contextualization of the gospel.

Process Item II: Ministry Task
(Resolution of Conflict at Highest Authority Level)

To settle the issue, the church appointed Barnabas and Paul to go together to see the apostles. It is worthy to note that the church picked its own people in whom they had confidence regarding the Gentile ministry to put the question before the Jerusalem Council.

Paul's ability to push out theological frontiers in the understanding of truth was evidently confirmed by Barnabas, for together they journeyed to the Jerusalem Council. And more importantly, Barnabas became the bridge between Jewish Christianity and the new understanding which expanded to include Jerusalem to bridge back to the Jewish Christianity base. The Jerusalem Council accepted the contextualization of the gospel, thus paving the way for a vast expansion of Christianity.

When Paul and Barnabas returned to Antioch, they taught the church along with a number of other leaders. But it is likely now that the church grappled with the cross-cultural implications of the gospel and with function more than with form.

Process Item III: Linking

Barnabas and Paul forced an apostolic gathering to resolve the issue at stake. It was here that Barnabas performed his final linking function. It was probably because Barnabas had greater credibility with the Jerusalem Council than did Paul, that once again in Jerusalem, Barnabas took the lead. (Note Acts 15:12, where the usual Paul-and-Barnabas address is reversed to Barnabas and Paul). The confirmation by this apostolic gathering gave final release to Paul, both in content and methodology, to evangelize the Gentile world. Barnabas' linking ministry as a mentor for Paul was essentially completed.

Sub-Phase C: Cyprus Church Development

The predominant process items of this sub-phase are:
1. Conflict (with Paul over second trip)
2. Mentoring (John Mark)
3. Sphere of influence

Process Item I: Conflict (with Paul over Second Trip)

Paul in his enthusiasm suggested to Barnabas that they return to the churches in Asia Minor where they had previously established churches to see how they were doing. Paul was no longer in need of mentoring, but Barnabas, ever the patient tolerant mentor saw potential in John Mark which should be developed and wanted to take him along.

Perhaps Barnabas wanted to act as a bridge between Paul and John Mark to overcome any hard feelings that might have occurred when John Mark had left the previous missionary journey. More likely, Barnabas was able to overlook John Mark's faults and was willing to help him develop. "Perhaps Barnabas could sympathize with John Mark the more easily because of his own weakness," that of "yielding to 'them of the circumcision'" in Galatians 2:11-14 (Ryley 1893:113).

Paul sharply objected to John Mark coming on this journey. An argument ensued which resulted in Paul and Barnabas going their separate ways. Each was probably partly right, for each had convictions, and partly wrong. Barnabas and John Mark return to Cyprus. We assume that they established churches there among those converts arising from the first missionary ministry task.

Process Item 2: Sphere of Influence

Once again Barnabas chose to take the route of less glory. ". . . when Barnabas and Paul separated and took up separate fields of missionary activity (Acts 15:39-41), Paul took the strategic road to Asia Minor, Greece, and Rome, while Barnabas went off to a field of lesser importance in Cyprus" (Filson 1940:85).

> . . . S. Luke shows no interest in the history of the mission at Salamis. The inference is that in fact S. Paul found very little work to do there for the reason that the synagogues were so little attended by Gentiles that they did not furnish any opening for reaching them. . . . Apparently there seemed no prospect of doing anything at Salamis but organizing the old converts and their disciples of Jewish origin into a Christian community and making a certain number of fresh Jewish converts (cf. Acts 11:19, where the evangelists in Cyprus are represented as speaking only to the Jews, not to the Greeks, as are those at Antioch) (Knox 1925:207).

From this point on the focus would be on Paul fulfilling his promised sense of destiny, and Barnabas would fade into the background as far as scripture is concerned.

We can infer that Barnabas' sphere of influence remained at a small national level (Cyprus), for if he had expanded his ministry, it most likely would have been the evangelization of the other Mediterranean islands. It seems clear that he did not, for Paul addresses his letter to Titus in terms of the island of Crete. However, Barnabas would have a large indirect sphere of influence through Paul.

We hear no more of Barnabas other than two indirect references. In I Corinthians, Paul mentions Barnabas in connection with teaching on apostleship and giving. From this mention three things can be assumed: 1) Barnabas was still involved in ministry, 2) Paul and Barnabas had at least made some bridging of their relationship, and 3) Barnabas was using a tent-making strategy in his apostolic role. A second mention in Colossians 4:10 shows that Barnabas' work with John Mark was not in vain. His mentoring function, particularly the discernment quality of seeing potential in yet-to-be-developed leaders, was vindicated.

Process Item III: Mentoring (John Mark)

At the time of this conflict Paul had not learned to be a mentor, and perhaps he did not have the gifts to be one. This may be borne out by Acts 15:41 where it is mentioned that Paul went through Syria and Cilicia "strengthening the churches." It seems that Paul was interested in strengthening churches/groups, while Barnabas was more interested in developing potential leaders/individuals. Ryley says that ". . . without wronging Paul, it may be fairly enough wished that he had remembered how once he needed a champion and friend, and had found both comforter and advocate in Barnabas" (1893:111). However, since Paul calls Timothy "my dear son" in II Timothy 1:2, it is possible that Paul did learn to be a mentor through imitation modeling, although the phrase could refer more to a conversion experience rather than mentoring.

Whether John Mark's reason for previously leaving Paul and Barnabas was lack of courage or because he objected to Paul's emerging leadership, it is little wonder that Paul did not want to take him along.

> Nevertheless, Barnabas clung to the belief that there were much greater possibilities in Mark than his past record suggested. . . . We need to remember, however, that Barnabas not only was a relative of Mark, but also was a man who all along and in varied situations had been marked by sympathy and understanding. It is not surprising, therefore, that he preferred to separate from Paul rather than give up the hope that Mark would yet prove of worth in the Christian enterprise (Filson 1940:109).

However, Barnabas' mentoring of John Mark paid off, for:

> The once weak comrade won his way to the very heart of Paul. Nothing could more tenderly evidence this than the fact that when he was a prisoner in Rome, Paul wrote most tenderly of

John Mark, as one of the 'men who have been a comfort to me.'
And later still, he longed for Mark's company – wanting him
even when he was anticipating the coming of his 'true child in
faith' – Timothy. To Timothy it was that Paul sent the message,
'Take Mark, and bring him with thee: for he is useful to me for
ministering" (Ryley 1893:116).

Table of Principles - Phase IV

NAME	OBSERVATION	PRINCIPLES (COMMENTS)
1. Completion Report	After completing their journey, Paul and Barnabas returned to Antioch and reported to the church all that God has done.	a. It is important to keep the support base informed of the ministry of their commissioned workers. b. Reporting back to the support base gives a sense of closure to a task.
2. Contextualization (Theory and Practice)	Previously the Jewish church had accepted the theory of accepting Gentiles, but when it came to eating with them and the question of circumcision, it was another matter.	a. It is extremely important that we live out our theory in our daily lives. Otherwise, we are no better than the hypocrites Jesus drove from the temple.
3. Apostolic Confrontation	When men from James came to Antioch, Peter quit eating with the Gentiles. Others were led astray, even Barnabas.	a. When establishing a new movement, error on the part of the main leadership needs to be confronted, for it can lead others astray. b. Encouragers/linkers/peacemakers need to be careful that these qualities do not cause them to follow error.
4. Information Distibution	On the way to Jerusalem Council, Paul and Barnabas shared what God had done among the Gentiles.	a. The workings of God need to be shared. b. By widely sharing what God has done, a Ċpower baseÓ can be established for future workings of the Lord.

Table of Principles - Phase IV Cont.

NAME	OBSERVATION	PRINCIPLES (COMMENTS)
5. Resolution of Conflict	Barnabas and Paul took the issue of circumcision and eating to the Jerusalem Council where Peter and James spoke in behalf of the Gentiles and it was decided these were not the key issues and only the key issues should be insisted upon.	a. In establishing a new movement, deciding what are the key issues to maintain the faith must be decided at the highest levels of authority. b. Having fallen into error, we need to do what we can to correct the problem (e.g. Peter) c. Flexiblity in moving from traditional positions need to be maintained in new and different situations. d. Once the issue is settled, the top leadership needs to send their guidelines to the community of faith.
6. Linker	Barnabas is well known to the Jerusalem Council and he lead in the report there. When the issue was settled, he also linked the Jerusalem Council's decision back to Antioch.	a. To be a good linker, the individual must have credibility in both the circles he/she seeks to link. b. It is important not only to link to the parent body but to link back to the home base.
7. Power Inherent in Team Ministry	Together Judas and Silas of Jerusalem ministered with Paul and Barnabas in Antioch and encouraged the church there.	a. There is one great power available in a team ministry. b. While one person may not have all the gifts necessary for a particular work, within the team God provides the gifts are usually there.
8. Conflict (with Paul)	When Paul proposed going on a second ministry journey, Barnabas sought to bring along John Mark. Paul strongly opposed this.	a. Championing a potential leader can create dissension in other relationships. b. Conflict can be a means of sending a mentoree out on his/her own.
9. Ministry Task (Takes Mark)	Barnabas took John Mark to Cyprus to build up the churches there.	a. Belief in a potential leader can provide a "second chance."
10. Mentoring (John Mark)	Barnabas's mentoring of John Mark paid off, for later Paul asks for Mark who has been helpful in his ministry.	a. Not all mentorees will progress at Paul's speedy rate; each need to be treated as an individual and given time to delvelop his/her potential. b. People who have not believed in the potential of a mentoree should be willing to reverse their opinion.
11. Indirect Sphere of influence	Barnabas provided a ministry experience for Paul. Her influenced Paul (e.g. giving). Barnabas's development of Paul paved the way for Paul's ministry. Barnabas had an investment in Paul which paid high dividends.	a. A mentor may accomplish more in the indirect sphere of influence through the potential leader than ever by direct ministry.

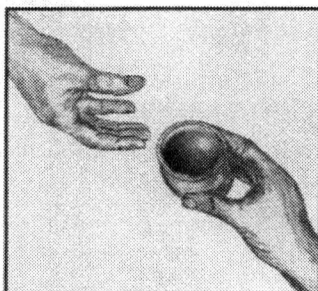

CONCLUSIONS
AS TO EXPECTATIONS

Laura

I feel that this study had led me into a much greater understanding of a little biblical character. For one thing, I was amazed at how much data can be extracted from what appears at first to be a rare mention of a biblical character.

The study also took the idea of mentoring out of the realm of theory (from reading the mentor sheet in *Leadership Emergence Theory*) and fleshed it out with real-life incidents. It also made me feel that I could attempt to mentor someone. Undoubtedly this is an area in which people need to grow as well as in the area of spiritual gifts.

In addition to learning about Barnabas and mentoring, I feel I also gained a greater understanding of the spiritual gift of encouragement (exhortation), one which I feel I have.

Already I have used Barnabas as an example of a mentor/encourager in a devotional and in individual conversations, and since Barnabas has now become "a part of my life," I am sure that over and over again this study will provide examples for me to share with people to encourage their own spiritual development.

Bobby

I listed five expectations at the beginning of this study. I probably gained the most insight concerning my first expectation on mentoring. I'll say a word on this in the contribution and major findings.

I went beyond my second expectation. In addition to fleshing out a biblical illustration of the gift of exhortation, which I feel was accomplished, I have seen Barnabas as a good biblical illustration of the apostolic gift. I will elaborate more on this in the section on contribution and major findings.

I believe we made a good start on the third expectation, that of providing a model (format-wise) for doing a midi-data LSP study. In addition to format I believe Laura contributed greatly to the academic credibility of the study by her library research. It is evident that she did a lot of homework and brought in insights from expert opinion. Previous LSP studies have done very little in the area of referring to expert opinion.

Expectations four and five have yet to be proved. The usefulness of the paper as well as its impact in the area of spiritual formation in the lives of students will be evaluated as I use the paper in my classes this year and next.

I have no doubt that the fifth expectation, that God will use this study of Barnabas to significantly impact spiritual formation, will be realized.

Important Findings from This Study

The important-findings section treats two kinds of contributions of the study. The first kind of contribution reflects on lessons seen in the study for present day readers. That is, how can our study of Barnabas' LSP contribute to our personal growth. The second kind of contribution attempts to evaluate how Barnabas impacted that part of the historical development of the Christian movement of which he was a part. This second kind of contribution is included on the Summary Sheet (see page 7).

Contributions for the Present Day

Five general items are worth noting for repeated emphasis from this study. These include:

1. Correlation of foundational factors with a major leadership selection decision;
2. Insights concerning apostolic ministry tasks and development of the apostolic gift;
3. Expanded thinking of the mentoring process item;
4. Some observations on bringing about change in the Antioch church; and
5. Expansion after response to word/obedience check process items.

In addition to these five general items, several principles are worth highlighting. These include:

Phase I.   Principle 1.   Sovereign Background (page 19)
Phase II.   Principle 1.   Exhortation Base (page 30)
Phase II.   Principle 2.   Early Lessons (page 30)
Phase IV.   Principle 3.   Apostolic Confrontation (page 48)
Phase IV.   Principle 4.   Information Distribution (page 48)
Phase IV.   Principle 5.   Resolution of Conflict (page 49)
Phase IV.   Principle 6.   Linker (page 49)
Phase IV.   Principle 11.   Indirect Sphere of Influence (page 49)

I will comment on each of the five general items first. Then I will make some comments on the principles listed above. Finally, I will say a concluding word on Barnabas and his major contributions to the Christian movement.

1. Correlation – Foundation Factors and a Major Decision

Some decisions in life are pivotal and swing us onward toward fulfillment of our sense of destiny. Such a momentous decision in Barnabas' life is covered over by the simple words of Acts 11:22. Note the context and the simple statement of fact (my italicizing for emphasis) dealing with a key decision that will eventually lead on to God's expansion of Christianity among the Gentiles.

> Now they which were scattered abroad upon the persecution that arose about Stephen travelled as far as Phoenicia, and Cyprus, and Antioch, preaching the word to none but unto the Jews only. And some of them were men of Cyprus and Cyrene, which, when they were come to Antioch, spake unto the Grecians, preaching the Lord Jesus. And the hand of the Lord was with them: and a great number believed, and turned unto the Lord. Then tidings of these things came unto the ears of the church which was in Jerusalem: and *they sent forth Barnabas, that he should go as far as Antioch.*
>
> Acts 11:19-22

In doing LSP studies it frequently occurs that one in maturity ministry or convergence can correlate foundational factors[13] after the fact.[14] It is more rare to see how these factors can be significant before the fact. One of the reasons for noting and defining the process items under foundational factors (contextual, family and conversion) is to stimulate thinking when boundary decisions[15] are to be made toward correlation of foundational factors. The context, family and conversion process items are very general. Careful analysis of these items for correlation to anticipated ministry may be pivotal in moving one toward fulfillment of a sense of destiny. On page 26, I discuss for Barnabas how contextual items and family items (as well as growth items) were most likely very important in the decision to send Barnabas to Antioch. My point

---

13. Process items are grouped under 5 major non-exclusive categories: foundational factors, guidance factors, ministry factors, maturity factors. See LET, p. 19.

14. Maturity ministry and convergence refer to general development phases. A generalized timeline includes: I. Sovereign Foundations, II. Inner-life Growth, III. Ministry Maturing, IV. Life Maturing, V. Convergence and VI. Afterglow.

15. Boundary conditions refer to the special processing which goes on during the times of transition from one sub-phase to another or from one phase to another.

here is that leaders in boundary conditions which are forcing ministry decision leading into the next sub-phase or phase should search back into their foundational factors as well as forward toward anticipated challenges. I believe some major decisions can be made with assurance when such correlation is seen.

2. Insights On Apostolic Ministry Tasks and the Apostolic Gift

A ministry task is defined as an assignment from God which primarily tests a person's faithfulness and obedience but often also allows use of ministry gifts in the context of a task which has closure, accountability and evaluation (Clinton 1984:42). Barnabas' trip to Antioch in Acts 11 is a classic example of a ministry task. An important thing to keep in mind about ministry tasks is that the ultimate assignment is from God whether or not the ministry task is self-initiated or assigned by another (as was the case with Barnabas). On the ministry task continuum the first facet of this ministry task occurs about mid-way as shown below.

◄────────────────	X ─────	──────────────►
Primarily For		Primarily For
Person Doing Task		Doing Task

It seems clear that Barnabas had grown greatly in spiritual authority within the church at Jerusalem, or he would not have been picked for this task. This ministry task would test Barnabas for a higher level of sphere of influence. As noted in Sub-phase C of Phase II on page 25, Barnabas actually went through a word check (i.e., could he apply what was learned in the Cornelius model to a new situation?). The function that the word check is testing is an apostolic function. Barnabas passed this test and went beyond. His spiritual authority was also attested to in the incident. Barnabas was ready for the most challenging aspect of the ministry task – to take what has been initiated in the work at Antioch and bring maturity to it. And this he did.

Principle 8, confirmation by apostles, (see page 31) points out two important selection principles:

8a. Spiritual leaders need to be sensitive to God's preparation in the lives of emerging leaders.

8b. Leaders need to respond to God's leading by entrusting responsibility to those God has selected for a task.

3. Expanded Thinking on the Mentoring Process Item

I expanded my thinking on mentoring by reflecting on four areas of Barnabas' mentoring activity.

The first area concerned the importance of linking. Barnabas was able to link in the following ways:

Situation 1: Between people (Paul to the Jerusalem elders);

Situation 2: Between a church and an unknown potential church (church at Jerusalem and the Antioch group);

Situation 3: Between a church and needed resources (Antioch church and Paul);

Situation 4: Between a church's corporate resources and needs of a group far away (marshalled financial resources from Antioch church for giving to the people of the famine at Jerusalem);

Situation 5: Between a mature church and cross-cultural gospel ministry needs (Antioch Church and lost Gentiles);

Situation 6: Between theological positions (Paul's advanced contextualized theology learned on missionary trips and the Jewish Christian theology at Jerusalem);

Situation 7: Between a young potential leader and needed experiential training (Mark and apprenticeship situations).

What does it take to link in these various situations?

Situation 1: The ability to see potential in a person who had a bad reputation, was abrupt and probably abrasive. Further, the ability to tolerate mistakes and patiently wait for development.

Situation 2: Credibility with the sending church was necessary. They had to be able to trust Barnabas' perceptions, insights and evaluations concerning the work at Antioch. Barnabas had to be able to gain spiritual authority fairly quickly with the group at Antioch in order to perform his mission of evaluation.

Situation 3: Barnabas needed a firm conviction that Paul would be helpful in the Antioch situation and that he could convince the Antioch church of Paul's usefulness. He needed determination to make the long trip to locate Paul and certainly a willingness to invest the time and money the trip would take. And most of all he had to be willing to work with Paul who was still young in formulating his theological convictions and had not had much church experience.

Situation 4: Barnabas believed in giving to meet needs. He also had to have discernment to know that this indeed was a word from the Lord. And he had to be able to convince others of these convictions.

Situation 5: A willingness to obey in the face of the unknown. A willingness to take a risk. A sense of destiny and the ability to sense God's voice.

Situation 6: Barnabas was most likely stretched by Paul's thinking on contextualization issues. Barnabas waffled at least once when some of Paul's ideas seemed so radical, although there were likely other reasons involved in his peace-keeping linking mentality which affected Barnabas' actions in the Peter controversy. Yet once he was convinced of his wrong he took a strong stand. He had maintained his credibility with the Jerusalem leaders. And he was able to bridge between the new and the old for he was a real part of both.

Situation 7: Barnabas saw the strain that the "authority switch" put on Mark. He knew that the change in authority and leadership was not what Mark had bargained for when he had been invited on the trip. So he overlooked Mark's decision to leave the team. He had genuine expectations for Mark and patiently paid the price to mentor him on to maturity even though it meant going against the strong-willed Paul and meant breaking up of an extremely successful ministry team.

Linking usually requires a person who can give and take and work between situations in order to bring about the necessary bridging. It will cost. Yet it is an extremely important means for indirectly influencing many things. One can get a feel for the importance of linking by considering "what if" thinking. Dale does this for Barnabas in the following quote.

> If Stephen hadn't prayed as he died, Paul might never have preached; but if Barnabas hadn't forgiven Paul's past and sponsored him within the Jerusalem church, Paul would never have had the chance to preach in the Jerusalem fellowship (Dale 1979:104).

Second, Barnabas gave John Mark a second chance at missionary work. Let's play a "what if" game. First, *What if* Barnabas hadn't guided Paul from a suspect outsider (Acts 9:26-30) to the leading missionary of the fledgling Christian movement? *What if* Paul had never been accepted into the Jerusalem and Antioch believer bands? Paul later wrote roughly one half of the New Testament. *What if* no Barnabas vouched for Paul? *What if* Barnabas hadn't stuck by his guns and insisted that John Mark be tried again? John Mark later wrote the earliest of the Synoptic Gospels. Not an eyewitness himself, Mark apparently wrote down the recollections of Simon Peter. No wonder Mark's account of Christ's ministry is so fast moving and vivid; Simon's impulsive nature and robust temperament are etched in every page. Wouldn't Christians today be missing a beautiful description of the words and works of Jesus if Mark had not set down the fast moving, "motion picture" Gospel?

> Mark's Gospel also influenced the later Synoptic Gospels. For instance Matthew uses 606 of Mark's 661 verses in his biography of Jesus. And Luke has 90 percent of Mark in it. *What if* Mark had not been given another chance to outgrow his early mis-

take? Of course, God could have used other persons and means to develop a New Testament record; but isn't it a wonder to see the stewardship of Barnabas' life, although he apparently never wrote a biblical line himself, in over half of the New Testament? *What if? What if?* Christians today can be certain that Paul and John Mark's contribution to the Christian faith was stimulated by Barnabas' ability to equip others to outgrow even Barnabas himself (Dale 1979:109-110; emphasis added).

Wagner further emphasizes the same ideas.

The most prominent biblical example of the gift of exhortation was Paul's associate, Barnabas, who was called "son of consolation" in Acts 4:36. It was Barnabas who took Paul under his wing when the other apostles were skeptical about the validity of his conversion. It was Barnabas who saw the potential in John Mark and picked him up when Paul had rejected him. As Leslie Flynn points out, "Do we realize that had not Barnabas used his gift of encouragement we might be missing half of the New Testament books?" Barnabas never wrote Scripture, but the people he helped did. Paul contributed 13 epistles, and Mark one Gospel (Wagner 1979:154).

Mentors who serve as linkers, such as Barnabas did, are needed today. Perhaps Barnabas' "behind the scenes" influence may serve as an example to spur many on to mentoring.

A second factor in Barnabas' mentoring that impressed me was his use of co-ministry not only as a training method but also as a way to increase the futuree's credibility, status and prestige. Barnabas did this with Paul and John Mark. To be willing to co-minister with a person who is less trained and has less spiritual authority requires a big person, for the majority of the benefits of such a relationship basically go one way. There is risk involved. For should the futuree not pan out, then the ministry and credibility of the mentor drops. And there is the further risk that if the futuree does do well and has the greater potential, he/she may well pass the mentor and not relate well to the former mentor. This brings me to the third thing I am impressed with in Barnabas' mentoring – the "authority switch principle."

Transition out of leadership is no easy matter. Many Christian organizations today can attest to the problems of replacing a leader. The "authority switch principle" was stated as a two part principle:

a. In mentoring a developing leader, one must recognize that he/she may surpass the mentor. At this point it may be necessary for the mentor to step down and to support the futuree from below in order to allow further development.

   b. At particular times God may choose to have a different leader, and the
       previous leader may be forced to stay on the scene. The previous leader
       needs to be humble and submissive in this changed situation.

Barnabas sets a beautiful example of transitioning from a position of direc-
tive leadership to one of supportive leadership. And he did it with class and in
such a way as to build up the leadership of his successor, Paul.

A fourth thing I noted in Barnabas' mentoring concerned his diversity in
mentoring. Principle 10 of Phase IV captures what I saw about this aspect of
Barnabas' mentoring. (See p. 49 for the observation event behind these principles.)

   a. Not All Mentorees Will Progress At Paul's Speedy Rate; Each Needs To
       Be Treated As An Individual And Given The Time To Develop His/her
       Potential.
   b. People Who Have Not Believed In The Potential Of A Mentoree Should
       Be Willing To Reverse Their Opinion.

Barnabas certainly was able to adjust the rate of training, kind of training,
relationships and anything else necessary to the mentoree concerned. In
Mark's case Paul did eventually reverse his opinion.

4. Some Observations on Bringing about Change in the Antioch Church

Apostolically gifted people see results. Barnabas saw results. From the brief
comments in Acts 11:19-30, we can surmise some of Barnabas' approach to
bringing about change. Barnabas was sent into a Gentile situation in order to
evaluate the genuineness of Christian expression. Obviously when he first
arrived he could have been critical of what he saw. For it is clear from his later
actions that there was much to do to in the church. But Barnabas was wise in
his approach to implementing change. Note his approach:

   1. He first affirmed that which he saw that was positive (11:23 "When he
       arrived and saw how God had blessed the people, he was glad.") He
       sensed the hand of God in it and confirmed that.
   2. He was opportunity-centered rather than problem-centered.[16] That is,
       he built upon the positive aspects that he first saw. Notice, he applies
       Goodwin's expectancy principle ("he. . . urged them all to be faithful
       and true to the Lord with all their hearts").
   3. He modeled a Christian life before the people and pitched into the min-
       istry and saw fruitfulness. (11:24: "Barnabas was a good man, full of

---

16. Havelock (1973) points out that change agents too often are problem-centered. He advocates
a three-fold analysis: opportunity analysis, problem analysis and systematic analysis. See Havelock's *The Guide To Innovation In Education*, the section on Diagnosis.

the Holy Spirit and faith, and many people were brought to the Lord.")

4. Barnabas had now attained credibility with the people. He had spiritual authority. He knew there was much to be done than he can do alone. So he became a resource linker and brought in Paul (11:25).

5. Because of his track record at Antioch, Barnabas was able to link in Paul and get him accepted as a person with ministry gifts (11:25).

6. Barnabas co-ministered with Paul for a year. During this year obviously many changes were implemented with excellent results. Note the evaluation wherein quantitative and qualitative growth are indicated (11:26: ". . . Taught a large group; it was at Antioch that the believers were first called Christians").

It is clear from 11:27-30 and 13:1-3 that Barnabas saw excellent results. There was a church which was sensitive to the Lord's leading. They responded to God's word. They were obedient. They had leadership. They would be an excellent base from which to launch a ministry into the Gentile world. Two important things should be noted. In Barnabas' approach to change he first built relationships.[17] He first accented the positive. Then he began the corrective work. And he realized the necessity of waiting for the right time[18] to bring in the correctives needed.

Dale points out in his article on Barnabas the balance that Barnabas had. Such a balance made him a natural change agent. "An effective leader must integrate a concern for people and a concern for production" (1979:107). He demonstrates this point in his article the managerial grid introduced by Mouton and Blake. This is a tool used by present-day managers to assess along a vertical and horizontal axis their concern for task.[19] Barnabas was well balanced. Whereas Paul was primarily a catalyst change agent, it is clear that Barnabas' change agent roles were as process helper and resource linker.[20] Process helpers know the strategic importance of relationships and people. Dale again helps us to see this aspect of Barnabas' change agent skills.

---

17. Of the 50 or so change models of which I have some familiarity there is one commonality among them all. A major stage in the process always focuses on relationships.

18. Change dynamics theory (such as is taught in the School of World Mission of Fuller Theological Seminary) analyzes several different kinds of times. Intervention time (when to implement) is a key. Obviously, Barnabas had an intuitive grasp of intervention time.

19. The vertical axis (0 at bottom to 9 at top) displays concern for people. The horizontal axis (0 at left to 9 at right) displays concern for production. The ideal leader according to the grid approach is 9,9 since he/she maximizes both his/her concern for people and concern for production. Dale says Barnabas was a 9,9 leader.

20. Havelock (1973) lists 4 major change agent roles and points out their various contributions as well as weaknesses. The 4 major roles are catalyst, solution giver, resource linker and process helper.

Trust is the human dynamic that is basic to all ministry. The ability to build and maintain relationships is fundamental to leading people. There is no evidence in the Bible's references to Barnabas that he approached the Antioch fellowship in anything other than a brother-to-brother relationship. Barnabas ministered as a peer, a fellow pilgrim on the way. Barnabas never hid behind a role. He wasn't Jerusalem's "religious inspector" to check out and straighten out the new Christians at Antioch. Barnabas knew that people trust persons, not roles. He knew that groups generally put more confidence in a helping brother than a bossy father. Barnabas was trusted (1979:103).

Although catalysts are important in the change process, they are not the most important. Resource linkers, solution givers and process helpers are also needed in the total process. And most important is the process helper. Barnabas was a process helper.

5. Expansion after Response to Word/Obedience Check Process Items

Leadership selection process theory identifies three recurring process items called word checks, integrity checks and obedience checks. Usually one thinks of them in terms of God's processing of individuals. Usually the checking process items are growth tests; individuals go through these processes and are tested by God. And usually there is an expansion of ministry upon proper response and growth. Now what is true for individuals is sometimes true for corporate groups. Such is the case with the Antioch church. Note carefully Acts 11:27-30. In this passage a local church went through a word check and an obedience check. Agabus gave a prophecy concerning a famine. They responded by ascertaining that the work was really from the Lord. And they obeyed it by determining that each of the people in the church would send as much as they could to help out. They sent Barnabas and Paul as representatives to Jerusalem. This function provided some further linking between this Gentile church at Antioch and the Jerusalem church. Further, it was during this visit that Barnabas and Paul were confirmed (received divine affirmation) of their apostolic ministry to the Gentiles. Then note that when they returned to Antioch (Acts 13:1-3) they were ready for the sense of destiny[21] experience that would impact the whole world. The church was ready. There was a support base from which to operate. The two leading actors were ready. Barnabas and Paul had ministered powerfully among Gentiles. They knew that they were Apostles to the Gentiles. And they knew that the church at Jerusalem, the center of the Christian movement, also recognized their apostleship. The time was

---

21. Sense of destiny is such an important process item in the development of upper level leadership that appendix pages are included treating it in depth.

right. And so the Holy Spirit moved. Expansion often follows word, integrity and obedience checks, apparently for corporate groups as well as individuals.

In addition to these five general items that I have just finished discussing I believe several principles are worth highlighting.

Phase I. Principle I. Sovereign Background (page19)

The Principle: Sovereign Base

Early details in a life often have long-term significance on major selection decisions.

I have already elaborated on this idea in the section correlating foundational factors but simply state it again for emphasis. Look back and sense the hand of God in the early details of life as you move toward convergence or make major decisions that will move you across boundaries into new development phases in your life.

Phase II. Principle 1. Exhortation Base (page 30)

The Principle: Exhortation Base

One who exhorts does so best out of personal life-changing experiences.

Barnabas' own sacrificial giving process item (Acts 4:36, 37) formed the basis for his authoritative teaching and influencing of Paul and the church at Antioch concerning giving. In the appendix is some information on developing the gift of exhortation. Appendix A-4, Step 1, procedure 2, applies the above principle. Appendix A-5, Step 6, procedures 1, 2 and 3 also applies this principle. In studying the gift of exhortation (see Appendix A-2), I note that a person possessing this gift will normally be stronger in exercising one of the aspects of it. The three emphases of the gift include:

1. To urge or admonish;
2. To encourage;
3. To comfort.

In my opinion, Barnabas was strongest in aspect 2 of that gift.

Phase II. Principle 2. Early Lessons (page 30)

The Principle: Early Lessons

Leaders are often tested early-on with regards to obedience and finances. Responses to these will lead to expanded personal growth and ministry.

Generosity is catching. Barnabas was a generous man. He saw his finances as belonging to the Lord and available to the Lord whenever needed. A leader who learns this early in ministry can expect to model this and greatly influence followers toward the same kind of generosity. The church at Antioch was a generous and giving church. I expect that every church Barnabas ever worked in had that same spirit. Leaders who have trouble with finances in their churches perhaps need look no further than their own personal processing by God in the area of giving and finances in order to find the solution to the financial problems in their church.

Phase IV. Principle 3. Apostolic Confrontation (page 48)

I have modified the two original sub-principles under this heading and made them four. I will discuss these and point out their importance in my opinion.

The Principle: Apostolic Confrontation and Apostolic Unity

a. *When establishing a new movement, fundamental error on the part of the main leadership needs to be confronted. (Move toward the purity side.)*

b. *When establishing a new movement, disagreements on peripheral truth should be viewed flexibly. (Move toward the side of unity.)*

c. *Encouragers/ linkers/peace makers need to be careful that these qualities do not cause them to follow error. (They tend toward the unity side.)*

d. *Truth defenders/ those who need to always be right need be careful that being right does not bring more harm by splitting than the good it does. Being right orthapraxically is often just as important as being right orthodoxically. (They tend toward the purity side.)*

In his letter to the Galatians, Paul has this strong statement.

> But when Peter came to Antioch, I opposed him in public, because he was clearly wrong. Before some men who had been sent by James arrived there, Peter had been eating with the Gentile brothers. But after these men arrived, he drew back and would not eat with the Gentiles, because he was afraid of those who were in favor of circumcising them. The other Jewish brothers also started acting like cowards along with Peter; *and even Barnabas was swept along by their cowardly action.* When I saw that they were not walking a straight path in line with the

truth of the gospel, I said to Peter in front of them all, "You are a Jew, yet you have been living like a Gentile, not like a Jew. How, then, can you try to force Gentiles to live like Jews?" (Good News Bible: Gal 2:11-14; emphasis added).

All of the principles listed above are drawn from this strong passage. Maintaining unity and maintaining purity are both strong desiderata in Christianity. Often these are at two ends of a continuum. Some people tend toward one end or the other of that continuum as a bent of life. Some are able to maintain a dynamic tension and hold both simultaneously. Giftedness, personality traits and experience seem to affect where a person comes down on the continuum. Observed traits or gifts such as exhortation (particularly the encouraging and comforting aspects), peace making, gentleness, relationship-orientation at the expense of the task all tend to put a person toward the maintaining-unity end of the continuum. Barnabas tended toward that end of the continuum. Two dangers need to be avoided. One cannot maintain unity at the expense of "core issues of truth." One can not afford to divide over every issue of truth on which there is disagreement. In this instance, the heart of the Gospel was at stake and Paul rightly comes down on the side of maintaining doctrinal truth. Barnabas, in my opinion, was not necessarily cowardly (as the Good News interprets) but was intent on bridging between Paul and Peter (or between Paul's new theological views and those of the older established Christians from Jerusalem). In this case I feel Paul, and not Barnabas, was operating more properly along that important truth/unity continuum. Thus the importance of the two principles given above. Later in regards to the conflict which split Barnabas and Paul, I feel Barnabas was operating more properly along that important truth/unity continuum.

Phase IV. Principle 4. Information Distribution (page 48)

The Principle: Information Distribution

a. *When the workings of God are shared they often bring fresh outbreaks of like results in the new setting in which they are shared.*

b. *By widely sharing what God has done, a "power base" can be established for future workings of the Lord.*

In Acts 13 and 14 wherever Paul and Barnabas went they "exchanged information." They recounted what had happened to them and how the Lord had met them.

> When they arrived in Antioch, they gathered the people of the church together and told them about all that God had done with them and how he had opened the way for the Gentiles to believe (Acts 14:27).

> They were sent on their way by the church; and as they went

through Phoenicia and Samaria, they reported how the Gentiles had turned to God; this news brought great joy to all the believers (Acts 15:3, 4).

When they arrived in Jerusalem, they were welcomed by the church, the apostles, and the elders, to whom they told all that God had done through them (Acts 15:4).

The whole group was silent as they heard Barnabas and Paul report all the miracles and wonders that God had performed through them among the Gentiles (Acts 15:12).

Paul uses this technique of information distribution or "cross-fertilization" in many of his letters. He will describe how other churches and people have done things and use them as motivating points along Goodwin's expectancy principle. I elaborate more on this whole information distribution principle in my unpublished paper, "Prayer, Recrudescence, and the Cross-fertilization Effect." In it I state the information distribution principle as,

> Wide dissemination of facts, about movements of God or God's increased recrudescence efforts, greatly increases the rate of recrudescence and ultimately generates more movements. (Clinton 1979:8).

I have since begun to study the importance of this principle as it applies to the indirect sphere of influence power base.[22] The effect of writings, conferences, seminars, workshops and radio ministries all build on this important principle. In his course at the School of World Mission, The Historical Development of the Christian Movement, Dr. Paul E. Pierson lists several themes which reoccur in bringing about the expansion of Christianity. One of those has to do with this information distribution principle.

Phase IV. Principle 5. Resolution of Conflict (page 49)

The Principles: Resolution of Conflict

a. *In establishing a new movement, the key issues to maintain the movement must be decided at the highest levels of authority.*

b. *Once the issue is settled, the top leadership needs to communicate their guidelines to the community of the movement.*

I have noted in my experience with mission boards and churches that while the top leaders may know what has been decided and why, since they went through the process to arrive at the decisions it is often the case that the communication of the same to the grass roots level is lacking. Even when clear

---

22. See the appendix pages (A20-23) devoted to Lillie's sphere of influence. His display treats three power bases: supernatural, natural and indirect.

cognitive communication occurs (and this too is rare) the affective component of the decision is often lacking. Principle 8 of Phase IV (see page 49) also sheds some light on conflict and resolution.

The Principle: Conflict between Individuals

a. *Championing a potential leader can create dissension in other relation-ships.*

b. *Conflict can be a means of sending a mentoree out in his/her own.*

In light of Dale's comments which follow and the principles of change advocated by Lyle Schaller,[23] I would add a third principle.

c. Seek to resolve conflict so both sides move positively ahead.

Note Dale's comments along these lines.

> When Barnabas and Paul disagreed over John Mark's place in the second missionary journey, they were direct in expressing their conflict. There was a "sharp connection" (Acts 15:39, RSV) between them. Rather than allow their disagreement to short-circuit the missionary enterprise, they looked for and discovered a win/win situation. They created two missionary teams! Barnabas and Paul apparently knew that conflict can be resolved in two destructive manners; win/lose and lose/lose. In a family-style community like the church, any losing resolution damages the climate and motivational level of the entire congregation. The win-win possibility was best of all. There's a forceful principle in this heated encounter between these two Christian giants: Disagreement won't damage Christian ministry if Christian leaders keep the redemptive purpose of God constantly in sight (1979:110-111).

I think Dale was a bit kind on Barnabas and Paul in saying that they apparently knew about win/win solutions. But whether they did or did not is not the important issue. The end result of their actions was a win/win solution. And there is the inherent principle now seen in hindsight.

---

23. Schaller (1972) treats conflict as a positive dynamic in his approach to change. See *The Change Agent*, pages 166-169, where he gives numerous suggestions on conflict and change.

Phase IV. Principle 11. Indirect Sphere of Influence (page 49)

The Principle: Indirect Sphere of Influence

A mentor may accomplish more in the indirect sphere of influence through the potential leader than ever by direct ministry.

A mentor is a special category of a divine contact. It may well be that the mentor's sense of destiny is more linked with making those crucial divine contacts and linking them on to their further development than it is with any special accomplishments or tasks. In any case, Barnabas in influencing Paul and John Mark at crucial times in their lives, influenced many others of whom you and I are a part.

As to Barnabas' Contributions to the Christian Movement

We have looked at some of the contributions of this study to our present day thinking. What remains now is to say a word concerning the contributions of Barnabas to the Christian movement. We will do this by discussing his sphere of influence and then summing up his contribution along the lines of linking.

Barnabas' Sphere of Influence per Development Phase

It is very difficult to discern what Barnabas' sphere of influence was in the first phase of his life. Presumably he was a pious person, being a Levite, and therefore, he probably had some influence at the local synagogue.

When Barnabas appeared upon the scene in Acts 4:36 (Phase II-A), he had a very limited sphere of influence. It was on the local level within the Jerusalem church. Phase II-B reveals that Barnabas was well respected within this circle.

When the Jerusalem church sent Barnabas to Antioch (Phase II-C1), his influence switched to another local church, although he still maintained enough credibility with the Jerusalem church that they were apparently willing to accept his judgment regarding the conversion of Gentiles.

Near the end of this second phase, Barnabas and Paul took the famine offering from Antioch to Jerusalem and therefore provided inter-church contact, thus slightly expanding his sphere of influence.

Upon arriving in Cyprus on the first missionary journey (Phase III-A2), Barnabas' influence expanded to the bi-national level. Then as they continued on their journey into Asia Minor (Phase III-B), his sphere of influence expanded to the multi-national level. By the third section of Phase III-B, Christian fellowships were forming, rather than just individual conversions, and Barnabas of course had influence with these groups.

Then in Phase III-C, churches were beginning to form. Paul and Barnabas appointed elders for these churches, and so Barnabas' influence now reached to multi-national churches.

Barnabas' multi-national direct sphere of influence continued through IV-B. But then the conflict arose with Paul over taking John Mark on the next missionary journey. Barnabas opted for service in Cyprus where he could mentor John Mark, and his direct sphere of influence was reduced to that national level within the churches of Cyprus.

However, although Barnabas' direct sphere of influence was reduced at this point, his previous mentoring of Paul greatly increased his indirect sphere of influence as Paul moved out into new areas of the Gentile world.

General Remarks

Barnabas ". . . Contributed immensely to the progress of the early Church," especially in three areas: in practical helpfulness, as a bridge between Jew and Gentile and in finding and developing new leaders (Filson 1940:90). He was "a good man, full of the Holy Spirit" who modeled a lifestyle before the Christian community that they could emulate. He was a great encourager, a flexible person, someone who was able to accept what God was doing in new ways, a patient person who could overlook the mistakes of others, and someone who was humble enough to be able to step back out of the limelight and in so doing, allow another person to develop.

Barnabas is the New Testament's archetype of a mentor.

> Especially in his success in developing a leader out of a failure, Barnabas becomes an almost perfect representative of the worthy Christian leader. What is the gospel but a second chance for us all? Not only in drawing out the best that lies in people, not only in developing in such people possibilities which perhaps they themselves do not see, but even more in aiding them to overcome their record of failure and in leading them in to a life of usefulness, the Christian leader does a great work (Filson 1940:112-13).

And so Barnabas passes from the pages of the New Testament. He was born into a contextual situation which fitted him to be a natural bridge to the Gentile world. By gifts, training, growth and temperament he was divinely suited to link Christianity to the Gentile world. His exhortive, apostolic gift-mix was greatly used by God "unto its full measure of faith."[24]

---

24. See footnote 10.

In his sermon on Barnabas, "A New Testament Good Man," George Truett, the famous Baptist preacher, develops in some detail the Ultimate Testimony[25] of Barnabas. He comments in the closing exhortations of his sermon,

> Long enough have I spoken. One more word. We can not all be great men like Paul. None of us can. But we can be good men like Barnabas. We can be good men. Oh brethren, to be good men, that is the first thing in the Kingdom of God! Genuine goodness – not cleverness, not smartness, not intellectuality, but goodness – that is the fundamental thing in the Kingdom of God. We may not be great. We may not sway the multitudes. We may not have our pictures in the paper. There may not be written editorials about us. But we can be good men (Truett 1915:90, 91).

It would be fitting, then, to end our study on Barnabas by closing with the Bible comment on which Truett developed Barnabas' Ultimate Testimony.

> Barnabas was a good man, full of the Holy Spirit and faith, and many people were brought to the Lord. (Acts 11:24)

Might we wish that each of us could have a fresh vision of the possibility of unselfishly developing people as Barnabas did. The four essentials of Barnabas' Ultimate Testimony are worthy to be modeled (Heb. 13:7, 8).

---

25. Ultimate Testimony refers to the phraseology used to evaluate the "bent of life" contribution of a leader to the Christian cause after that leader has passed from the scene.

BARNABAS

ENCOURAGING EXHORTER

APPENDICES

Mentoring Process Item
Mentor Synonym: Sponsor

Introduction	God has given some people the capacity and the heart to see leadership potential and to take private and personal action to help the potential leader develop. That action usually becomes a form of significant guidance for the potential leader.
Definition	*Mentoring* refers to the process where a person with a serving, giving, encouraging attitude (the mentor) sees leadership potential in a still-to-be developed person (the futuree or protege) and is able to promote or otherwise significantly influence the futuree along to the realization of potential.
Definition	*A mentoring process item* refers to the process and results of a mentor helping a potential leader.
Bible Example	Barnabas mentored Saul. Barnabas also mentored John Mark, a New Testament author.
Historic Example	Margaret Barber mentored Watchman Nee. Her mentoring included informal apprenticeship and imitation modelling.
Historic Day Example	Charles Trumbull was an important mentor for Robert C. McQuilkein, the founder of Columbia Bible College.
Present Day Example	John Stott has found ways to send several emerging leaders for further training and other experiences which undoubtedly have broadened their sphere of influence.
Mentor Characterisics	• can readily see potential in a person, • can tolerate mistakes, brashness, abrasivness, etc. in a person in order to see potential develop, • is often a very flexible person, • is patient, recognizing that it takes time and experience for a person to develop, • has vision and ability to see down the road and suggest next steps that a futuree needs for development, • usually has a gift-mix including one or more of the encouragement spiritual gifts: mercy, giving, exhortation, faith, word of wisdom.

Ways
Mentors
Help
Futurees

- giving timely <u>advice</u> which encourages the futuree,
- <u>risking</u> his/her reputation in backing the futuree,
- <u>bridging</u> between the futuree to needed resources,
- <u>modelling</u> and using Goodwin's Expectation principle,
- <u>giving</u> tracts, letters, books or other literary information which opens perspectives for the futuree,
- <u>giving</u> financially, sometimes sacrificially to further the futuree's ministry,
- allowing <u>co-ministry</u> which will increase the futuree's credibility, status and prestige,
- having <u>freedom</u> to allow end even promote the futuree beyond the mentor's own level of leadership.

Exhortation

Introduction   Much information is given in the New Testament about the gift of exhortation. We know that it is a distinct gift and *not* simply a part of the gift of prophecy since both are listed in Romans 12 seperately. Many illustrations of this gift abound in the epistles, showing that its function is very important to the life of the church.

Background
Word Studies On Exhortation

Greek Word	Etymological or Literal Use	Basic Idea	Contextual Verification
parakaleo	to call to a person	1. to beseech or admonish one to pursue some specific course of conduct in the future	Acts 2:40 Romans 15:30 Romans 16:17 I Cor. 1:10 II Cor.9:5 I Thess. 4:1 Heb. 1:25
		2. to comfort one in terms of some trial being experienced or already experienced	II Cor. 1:4 Eph. 6:22 Col. 4:8 I Thess. 4:18 I Thess. 5:11
		3. to encourage generally in order that people might face future events which may arise	Acts 11:23 Acts 14:22 I Cor. 14:31

Definition   The *gift of exhortation* is the capacity to urge people to action in terms of applying Scriptural truth, or to encourage people generally with Scriptural truth, or to comfort people through application of Scriptural truths to their needs.

Comments   A person possessing this gift will normally be stronger in exercising one of the aspects of it:
- to urge or admonish
- to encourage
- to comfort

However, full development of the gift will see all aspects of the gift used both privately and publicly.

Example of Exhortation Urging to Action	*"Now I urge* you bretheren, by our Lord Jesus Christ and by the love of the Spirit to strive together with me in your prayers to God for me" Romans 15:30
Example of Exhortation Encouraging Others	"Then when he had come and witnessed the grace of God, he rejoiced and began to *to encourage them all with* resolute heart to remain true to the Lord" Acts 11:23
Example of Exhortation Comforting Others	"Blessed be the God... the Father of mercies and God of all comfort who comforteth us in all our affliction, that we may be able to comfort them that are in any affliction, through the comfort where we ourselves are comforted" II Cor. 1:3,4

Symptoms of of this Gift

- People generally react strongly (sometimes for and some times against) what you say.
- You frequently advise others to do this or that.
- You share a word with someone in need such that he takes the word as a comforting word from God.
- People frequently confide in you their innermost problems because they sense in you an empathic ear and by such confiding are comforted.
- People like to be around you because you cheer them up simply by your attitude and demeanor.
- You often sense an urgency to get something done and are willing to transmit this urgency to others.
- You love to share with anyone a truth from a verse of Scripture which has meant much to you.
- You are not satisfied with a superficial acceptance of truth but seek to have people actually use it.
- You enjoy sharing particular aspects of your testimony with others because you know God will use it in the lives of others.

Uses   The gift of exhortation is the major way through which God allows the body to enable each other to live practical Christians. Christians encourage each other to face trials by sharing what God has done for them in similar situations. Christians urge each other to action in terms of practical application. Chritians are encouraged to look forward to what lies ahead. These kinds of things take place when the exhortive gift is exercized on a one-to-one basis, a one-to-few, few-to-one, one-to-many basis. It is a gift which quite a few people in any given assembly can expect to have and should use.

How to Develop The Gift of Exhortation

Introduction   Each of us in the body of Christ needs to be encouraged and yes, sometimes prodded along as we live out our Christian lives. At other times, we especially need to be comforted. God has given the gift of exhortation within the body to meet these needs. The gift of exhortation is a primary means whereby Christians are enabled by one another to live Christ-like lives amidst their everyday circumstances. This gift should be the gifts of many in the body. In a number of the reciprocal commands we are told to exhort one another. The practical suggestions to develop this gift are based on using Scriptural patterns of exhortation as a guide for us in exercising this gift.

Assuming that you have the gift of exhortation and want to develop it...

Step	Procedure	Procedural Follow-Up
1.	Study regularly the passages of Scripture which are heavy in application.	1. Your regular Bible reading program should focus on these kind of passages. Your devotional life should focus on Scriptures which are applicational in nature. See Table of Passages Focusing on Application of Truth to Life, p. A-7. 2. Seek to apply these scriptures to your own life. Write down your personal applications and note your personal obedience to God. 3. Be particularly sensitive to the Holy Spirit. He will often quite often emphasize Scriptures which will apply to current situations around you.
2.	Study Bible books which will help you become sensitive to people's needs.	1. Read regularly in the Psalms and note: • The moods and changing experiences faced by people as they walk with God. • God's method of meeting people in these situations. • How you can use the various Psalms to bring comfort to those facing the same kind of situations. 2. Study Job to note: • How to and how not to empathize with those in suffering. • The stress on the sovereignty of God - this will be a foundational principle in comforting and encourageing people. 3. Study Ecclesiastes to see areas in which people seek satisfaction.

Step	Procedure	Procedural Follow-Up
3.	Use extra-biblical sources which will help you become sensitive to people's needs.	1. There a number of popularized books dealing with applied psychological principles and interpersonal relationships. Use these to help you learn to be sensitive to others and their needs. 2. Be careful to compare suggestions from extra-Biblical sources with scriptural principles where dealt with by the Bible.
4.	Memorize verses which will prove helpful to you as you use your exhortive gift.	Examples Proverbes 9:8, 10:17, 11:14, 15:28,31, 17:10, 20:5, 25:11,12, 26:4,5, 27:5,6,9,17 John 14:26, 16:13, II Cor. 1:3,4, 12:9 Hebrews 10:24,25, James 1:22
5.	Make sure you are clear on an approach to apply Scripture	1. People will question you on how you know such and such is true and applies to the situation. 2. Set forth your approach to recognizing truth from Scripture and using it in current situations. 3. Make sure you have an approach to disputed practices and Christian liberty since you will exercise your gift many times in regard to these areas.
6.	In Small Group Discussions and individual conversations be alert to promptings by the Holy Spirit in which he will call your attention to situations or problems to which he has previously given you help. Share these.	1. The experience you will face will be particularly used of God to teach you lessons to be used with others. 2. You will find that you are unusually sensitive to lessons learned from other's experiences also. You will also notice quick recall of verses, past experiences, and principles from time to time in your discussion with others. 3. Share these with others always in in love and with th principles of Phil. 3:15-16 in mind.
7.	Take advantage of opportunities in small groups and the gathered church to share your current experiences with God.	1. Because of the nature of your gift you can expect an unusual sensitivity to God in every day circumstances. 2. Your sharing of your everyday experiences will be used by God to meet others facing similar situations though you may not be aware of their situation. 3. Share in a God-centered way rather than an experience-centered way.

Table of Passages Focusing on Application of Truth to Life

Books or Passages	As You Read or Study You should Focus on:
Proverbs	• practical advice for all kinds of daily living • verses telling how to give advice • truth for current situation
Parables	• various central truths taught be each parable, most of these are fundamental principles of Christianity • Jesus' method in applying truth to situations • truth for current situations
Other Discourses in Gospels	• Jesus' method in applying truth to situations • truth for current situation
Romans 12-16	• principles of interrelationships between Christians • principles concerning disputed practices • principles concerning government • truth for current situation
I Cor.	• The entire book illustrates Paul's approach to various problems. Note principles for applying truth to problems. • truth which can be applied today
Gal. 1:6-10 2:1-21 3:1-5 5:13-6:10	• intensity needed when correcting serious problems • importance of taking a stand is essential truth is involved • fervor in admonishing and example of admonishing • truth for current situation
Eph. 4:1 Eph. 6:23	• examples of exhortive teaching • truth the content to apply to today's situation
Phil.	• how to share from your present experience so as to meet needs of others • exhortations to unity • truth for current situation
Col. 3,4	• examples of admonitions • truth for current situation

Books or Passages	As You Read or Study You should Focus on:
Heb. 2:1-4 3:7-4:13 5:11-6:20 10:26-39 12, 13	• examples of admonition • the importance of prefacing admonition by teaching • truth to apply to current situation
James	• practical use of Scripture to life situation • use and misuse of tongue • description of practical wisdom and principles for applying it • truth for current situation
I Peter	• how God expects us to submit to him in various areas of our lives and hence have our faith strengthened • various areas of life that need to be brought into subjection • truth to apply to apply to current situation
I,II,III John	• attitudes towards sin and truth • practical expressions of love • truth to be applied to current situation
Jude	• examples of strong warnings • truth to be applied to current situation

Comment   While the above are not all the exhortive or applicational type of passages in the Scripture, they are certainly representative of the kinds of passages that one with an exhortive gift ought to be reading, studying and using regularly.

Though the passages were listed to point out the location of exhortive or application Scripture, bear in mind that these passages, as all passages in Scripture, should be read in light of the context of the book as a whole of which they are a part.

Apostleship

Introduction   Some would **not** classify apostleship as a gift but would confine it to an office filled by those who were handpicked by Jesus to function in a foundational role in instigating the church. One holding this view would say then that with the passing away of the twelve (most would include Paul as a special case) this function ceased to exist. Others would agree that there was a special office called apostleship which did in fact exist only in New Testament times and that this office was filled by the original 12 and Paul. They would agree that this office did cease with the death of the 12 and Paul. However, they would add that there is an apostleship gift distinct from the original authoritative apostolic office. This gift continued beyond the first century. There is ample evidence that there was a functional apostolic role filled by a number of named individuals in Scriptures beyond Paul and the Twelve which does in fact meet the requirement of a gift of apostleship.

Basic Words
Studies   On Apostleship

Greek-Transliteration	Etymological or literal rendering	Basic Idea	English Translation	Contextual Confirmation
apostolos	one sent forth apo, from + stello, to send	one who acts authoritatively for another	apostle messenger	Heb.3:1 Luke 6:13, 9:10 Acts 14:4,14 Romans 16:7 II Cor. 8:23 Phil. 2:25 I Thess. 2:6
apostole	a sending	a mission a ministry	apostleship	Acts 1:25 Romans 1:5 I Cor 9:2 Gal. 2:8

Definition   The gift of apostleship refers to a special leadership capacity in which one exerts influence over others so as to establish new local churches and new works needed to enhance the spread of Christianity. Further, this gift functions to guide these new works in their foundational stages.

Explanation   The capacity to establish new local churches and other necessary Christian structures necssitates a special kind of authority.

Apostleship (cont.)

This is sometimes referred to as a "call" from God. The one having this special authoritative influence is usually recognized by local church as having authority from God to perform the task of pioneer work. The gift can be exercised within ones own culture or cross-culturally. Traditionally the apostolic gift has been associated with missionary work since its pioneer-quality was immediately evident. However, all who "go" as missionaries certainly don't have this gift, and many who "stay" should recognize this gift and apply it to "pioneer situations" within their own locality.

Examples
Acts 13:1-3 "Now there were in the church that was at Antioch certain prophets and teachers; as Barnabas, and Simeon that was called Niger, and Lucius of Cyrene, and Manaen, which had been brought up with Herod the tetrarch and Saul. As they ministered to the Lord, and fasted, the Holy Spirit said, "Separate me Barnabas, and Saul for the work *whereunto I have called them.* And when they had fasted and prayed, and laid their hands on them, they sent them away."
Note Barnabas as well as Paul was included in this apostolic gift.

Acts 14:4, 14 "But the multitude of the city was divided: and part held with the Jews, and part with the *apostles.* Which when the apostles, Barnabas and Paul, heard of, they rent their clothes, and ran in among the people, crying out,..."

Acts 14:22, 23 "Confirming to the souls of the disciples, and exhorting them to continue in the faith, and that we must through much tribulation enter into the kingdom of God. And when they had *ordained them elders* in every church, and had prayed with fasting, they commended them to the Lord, on whom they believed."

Negative
example
II Cor. 11:13 "For such are *false prophets,* deceitful workers, transforming themselves into the *apostles* of Christ." The value of this passage is that it implies there are many who were exsercising this gift (though some were not true apostles).

Example
establishing
leadership
Titus 1:5 "For this cause left I thee in Crete, that *thou* shouldest *set in order* the things that are wanting, and *ordain elders in every city,* as I had appointed thee:"

Apostleship (cont.)

Example | I Thess. 2:6 "Nor of men sought we glory, neither of you, nor yet of others, when we have been burdensome, as the *apostles* of Christ."
This use of apostles refers to Paul and Silvannus and Timothy.

Example | Rom. 16:7 "Salute Andronicus and Junia, my kinsmen, and my fellow prisoners, who are of note among the *apostles*, who also were in Christ before me" (note: Junia might possibly be a woman's name).

Use |
- founding of new church structures: it is through this sending-forth effort of selected individuals by established churches that new churches are founded. The individuals thus selected for this role must sense the God-given ability for this role as well as those doing the sending forth.
- founding of new mission structures: it is through apostolic gifted people that God has historically raised up structures to spur on the mission movement and to bring renewal into church structures which have lost their vision.

Symptoms |
- A strong sense of call by God for establishing new works.
- An equally strong confirmation by the local church of which you are a part.
- A forceful personality which can trust God to do what is necessary in unusual situations in order to establish authority for God's work.
- Usually will be a multi-gifted person having one or more other leadership gifts beyond apostleship.
- Ability to face new situations.
- A clear understanding of the nature of the church and its purpose.
- A personality which attracts people to follow (usually forceful).
- A person who can sense what God wants to do and is *not* afraid to try.
- A drive within which cannot be satisfied apart from seeing people presently unreached being reached and included in a community of God's people.

Special comment | Watchman Nee holds a distinct view concerning this gift (which he would call an office). For a view worthy of thought see his book *The Normal Christian Church Life*, p. 17 ff.

How to Develop the Gift of Apostleship

Introduction   E. M. Bounds said, "We are constantly on a stretch, if not on a strain, to devise new methods, new plans, new prganizations to advance the church and secure enlargement and efficient for the Gospel. This trend of the day has a tendency to lose sight of the man or sink the man in the plan or organization. God's plan is to make much of the man, far more of him than of anything else. Men are God's method. The church is looking for better methods; God is looking for better men." This is the essence of the gift of apostleship – one sent from God; one who will reach peoples for Christ and begin new churches, whither in the ghetto, the city, suburbs or rural areas, home or abroad; one who is willing to sacrifice, if necessary, to get the job done. We echo with E. M. Bounds – people are God's method. The essence of the apostolic function is a person called of God who has the capacity to begin works of God. He/she will usually be multi-gifted. The suggestions below are general and help develop background needed for a person through whom God can exercise the gift of apostleship.

Given you have the gift of apostleship and want to be developing yourself for greater use...

Step	Procedure	Procedural Follow-Up Suggestions
1.	Develop a clear understanding of the nature of the Church, its purposes, functions, and growth processes.	1. Do a formal or informal course of study to determine your Biblical view of the church. 2. Associate yourself with someone now being used of God in the Church Renewal movement and study and discuss with him concerning Biblical views of the Church. 3. Spend time with colleagues of like mind in exchanging ideas on the church.
2.	Be an all-around Bible student but master by in-depth studies special passages.	1. You should master the pastoral epistles. 2. You should master the church epistles. 3. You should master the selected leadership passages from other portions of Scripture. 4. You should read the book of Acts.
3.	Make a special study of the Spiritual qualifications of an elder and apply these standards to your own life.	1. You **must** model these standards. 2. You will use these standards to select leadership for the church you are founding.

Step	Procedure	Procedural Follow-Up Suggestions
4.	Develop a mind-set for strategizing.	1. Learn skills of goal setting, prioritizing, planning and evaluating. Then develop a very flexible attitude which can recognize the Spirit's confirmation or setting aside of plans. 2. Study the revival movements in church history to draw out the principles which can be reapplied. 3. Study the major movements in missions in the last 30 years: church growth, saturation evangelism, theological education by extension, church renewal, lay involvements, etc.
5.	Read widely.	1. Learn to read selectivly. 2. Read books on ecclesiology. 3. Read books on church growth. 4. Read books on personal renewal. 5. Read missionary biographies. Look for: a challenge from God, examples of God giving people vision, principles of building a work of God. 6. Read books in applied anthropology and sociology. More and more Christian authors and groups are writing in this field.
6.	Get on-the-job training with experts.	1. Find a church whic is demonstrating the philosophy of the church which you have come to undertsand. Ask God to open a way for you to move in to a situation and be used in it. 2. Find a successful church planter who you feel is exercising the apostolic function and ask them to take you into their ministry for a period of traning.
7.	Work primarily in the regional church.	1. Make certain you are under authority from a local church. 2. Keep flexible so that God can move you to new places.

Related map see *Apostleship*, page A-9

Convergence Synonym: Role Match

introduction   In the leadership selection process study of people who have had wide ministries and impact upon a large sphere of influence an often observed condition is convergence. Briefly stated convergence is the "coming together" of a number of factors including assignment of roles, experience, use of gifts, so that a person can contribute toward the maximum potential for which God intended. In short, convergence refers to the "fit" of the right person for the right job at the right time.

definition   *Convergence* refers to a ministry situation for a given person which maximizes the following factors so that the person ministers more efficiently and effectively.

Convergence Factors

Factor: **Related to Convergence**

Gift-mix   The person's gift mix is well identified, developed and has been used in various ministry experiences *and* the person is increasingly choosing ministry priorities in terms of gift-mix and diminant gift.

Experience   The person's past experience (including development of gift-mix, lessons are learned from major process items, variety of assignments, etc.) relate directly to the present ministry.

Temperament   The person's responsibility in terms of people relationships is ideally suited to the person's temperament and present emotional maturity.

Sphere of   The person's role and ministry responsibility allow for the
influence   person to minister to the "sphere of influence groups" best suited to the person's gift-mix and present development state.

Role   The formal role assigned not only frees the person from restrictions to use the gift-mix but actually enhances the use of gift-mix.

Example   See Leadership Selection Process study Reader #1 – the paper on Fletcher Tink.

Convergence (cont.)

Comment   Read carefully Tink's introductory remarks which point out par-
               ticularly experience and role match (pages 3-6). Then scan his
               overall time-line to note how his varied experience "fit" in order
               to prepare his for his present assignment.

Biblical   Jephthah, the 9th Judge (charismatic crisis leader) is an Old
               Testament example of convergence. His third development
               phase in which he delivers Israel (those in Gilead and
               Manasseh) from the Ammonites demonstrates convergence.
               Role, experience, and natural abilities all converge in this third
               phase. Role and experience are especially prominent. Giftedness
               is less seen but is implicit.

Sense of Destiny Synonym: Divine Intervention

Introduction God often intervenes in the lives of leaders who will eventually rise to levels 4 and 5 in such a way as to inspire them to attempt great things for Him. These special unique interventions are touched with the sense of the mystical. This special kind of process item is called a "sense of destiny."

Definition A *sense of destiny* process item is a unique awe-inspiring experience
• in which God reveals Himself,
• to an obedient surrendered believer,
• in order to inspire/lead that person on to accomplish something special in his/her life-time.

Examples *Abraham* Gen. 12:1-3; 13:14,15; 15:1ff; 17:1; 18:1
(inner heart voice, audible vouce, vision, Angelic visitor)
Joseph Gen. 37:5, dream; Gen. 37:9, dream; 45:5, fulfillment
Moses Ex. 2:8, divine intervention "Take this child..." Ex. 3:2 supernatural phenomena (burning bush)
Jephthah Judges 10, 11 (crisis destiny)
Daniel (many – in word, vision, angelic beings)
Paul Acts 9; 22; 26; see especially Acts 26:15ff, vs 19 I did not disobey the vision

Summary: audible voice, deep conviction in the heart, dreams, visions, unusual occurence in nature, word

Others observed Surrender experience, prophetic utterance, integrity check, divine contacts, mystical presence of Christ, divine confirmation experiences

Comment Often related to a "call experience" but also related to "keeping on target confirmation experiences."

4 Principles 1. It is the living eternal Almighty God who gives a "sense of destiny." He can do anything He pleases. Note that the names of God in the Old Testament often come with a sense of destiny experience. We know God more deeply after a sense of destiny experience.

2. God looks for one who is willing to be obedient and used for God's purposes – to that kind comes a sense of destiny. Not all will have this.

3. The sense of destiny experience may be repeated more than once in a lifetime. Usually awe-inspiring and not easily forgotten. Sometimes it is mystifying and only seen later after time has passed. Some reasons for repeated sense of destiny experiences,

    a. to affirm/confirm that we are still going to be used

    b. to help our sagging faith

    c. to clarify further, to reveal intermediate steps

4. When God chooses you for His purposes, be obedient and believe that He will accomplish that destiny through you.

Four Marks of a Sense of Destiny
Four Suggestions Concerning A Sense of Destiny

Introduction   It is helpful to know some of the items that can help one iden-
tify sense of destiny experiences. The following are some suggestions toward that end.

Four Marks   When you have a "sense of destiny" experience (at least when
you become aware that it was such an experience),
1. You know experientially that the living God has touched you.

2. You believe He has something worthwhile for you to
accomplish in your life-time,

3. You obediently follow along as God carries you on to the
accomplishment of that destiny. He will do what He promises.

4. At the end of your life-time you can refoice in knowing your
life counted in the purposes of God.

Four Suggestions

Remember   In its essence, a sense of destiny is a deep inner recognition that
God is going to use you as an integral part of his purposes
whether in a small role or large role. It is that sense of God
being in it and the importance of it that makes a sense of destiny experience vital. Ask God to give you a sense of destiny no
matter the "size" of work you are in or your "giftedness."

Suggestion 1   Seek to confirm that inner call that what you are doing is right
on target and important to God's purposes for you and His
work. (When it is all said and done you want to know that
what you have given your life for has counted.)

Suggestion 2   Make your major decisions based on,
• your sense of destiny,
• your gift/mix,
• your role matched to gift-mix.

Suggestion 3   Expect God to repeatedly confirm your sense of destiny as He
moves you on to your maximum potential place on the sphere
of influence.

Suggestion 4   Concentrate on those things which build spiritual authority,
• word,
• life,
• prayer life,
• power
And leave promotion along the sphere of influence to God.

Sphere of Influence

Introduction   In the phrase "measure of faith" in Romans 12:3,6 is implied as
                  potential level of effective use of gifts varying according to
                  God's unique gifting of individuals. For the phrase "measure of
                  faith" is a figure of speech called metonymy (where faith
                  stands for gift and emphases the quality of exercise of the gift;
                  "measure" would imply a degree of quantity). Our definition
                  "sphere of influence" seeks to capture this idea. That is, some
                  people will influence more people with the use of their gifts
                  than will others. Each is exhorted to make a correct assessment
                  of themselves and their gifts and abilities and to use them for
                  God's glory and the benefit of Christians. The following defini-
                  tion is an attempt to evaluate the concept of measure of faith
                  from the perspective of leadership selection processes. The
                  leadership selection process is completed when a leader reaches
                  that maximum level for which he/she is gifted and is continu-
                  ously operating in convergence. Leaders and those developing
                  leaders should continuously seek to identify sphere of influence
                  and make selection and training decisions which challenge
                  trainees to reach their God-given ministry potential.

Definition   *Sphere of influence* refers to the totality of people being influ-
                  enced and for whom a leader will give an account to God.

Comment   The totality of people can be further refined to mean individu-
                  als or group(s) of people being directly influenced and for
                  which a leader has direct responsibility and for those people
                  who are indirectly influenced by that leader.

Linear   I have generally used a linear sphere of influence which is
criterion   graduated from left to right in terms of people being influenced.
                  The influence capacity increases from individuals on the
                  extreme left to international leaders on the extreme right. An
                  example of the linear contiuum is given below.

individuals	family	small group	church community	association of churches	regional	national	inter- national

Weakness   The linear breakdown does not show the various aspects of
                  sphere of influence. It is a general overall "estimate."

Lillie's
circular

In order to express the idea that a person can be influencing different groups at different levels, Terrie Lillie (Overseas Missionary Fellowship missionary to Taiwan) devised a circular plot for sphere of influence which has proven very helpful. The circular graph uses three major divisions (spiritual authority, natural power base, indirect power base) with several minor groupings under each division. The end result of Lillie's approach is a visible profile of sphere of influence. The plot can be applied to corporate groups as well as individuals as a means of evaluation.

Related info

Spiritual authority, Lillie's sphere of influence, convergence

Lillie's Sphere of Influence Display

Introduction

In order to express the idea that a person can be influencing different groups at different levels via different ways Terrie Lillie (missionary to Taiwan) devised a circular plot for sphere of influence. Notice that he is emphasizing three major influence means: a natural power base, a spiritual power base and a relational power base. I adapted his original circular graph to include several new aspects in the major categories. The end result of Lillie's approach is a visible profile of sphere of influence.

Table of Lillie's Sphere of Influence Components

Label	Explanation
Word	A spiritual authority power base component measuring a person's influence on others because of a personal authoritative use of the Word of God for life and ministry.
Life	A component of a spiritual authority power base which measures influence that a person has on others because of his/her personal walk with God.
Prayer	A component of a spiritual authority power base which measures influence that a person of God has on events and people because of an intimate prayer relationship with God.
Ministry	A component of a spiritual authority power base which measures influence of a person's direct ministry (use of spiritual gifts) with people.
Legal	An authority base identified by Weber in studies of various societies. Legal authority bases its legitimacy on rational grounds, appealing to laws that have been formed by the group involved. Followers express an impersonal loyalty to the leader's office rather than to his/her person. The leader's right to issue commands is based on rational laws rather than having personally earned the right.
Tradition	An authority base identified by Weber finding its legitimacy in the sanctity of traditions that leaders respect and follow meticulously. Loyalty though given personally is based on the leader's respect for tradition.
Charismatic	An authority base identified by Weber finding its legitimacy in the personal charisma of leaders. Exceptional character qualifies them to lead. Followers are loyal to them personally. Leadership may be irrational. Appeal is made to extraordinary gifts rather than to rational laws.
Advisory	A measure of a person's indirect ability to influence others using mentor-like techniques of advising.
Associational	A measure of a person's indirect ability to influence others because of relationships established through membership in different interest groups.
Informational	A measure of a person's indirect ability to influence others through broadcasting of ideas personally or otherwise. Teaching and writing are specific examples.
Other	A catch-all miscellaneous category which measures influence people exert through various means such as conference ministries, radio or TV ministries, membership in important committees, control of wealth, etc.

Development of Lillie's Sphere of Influence Components

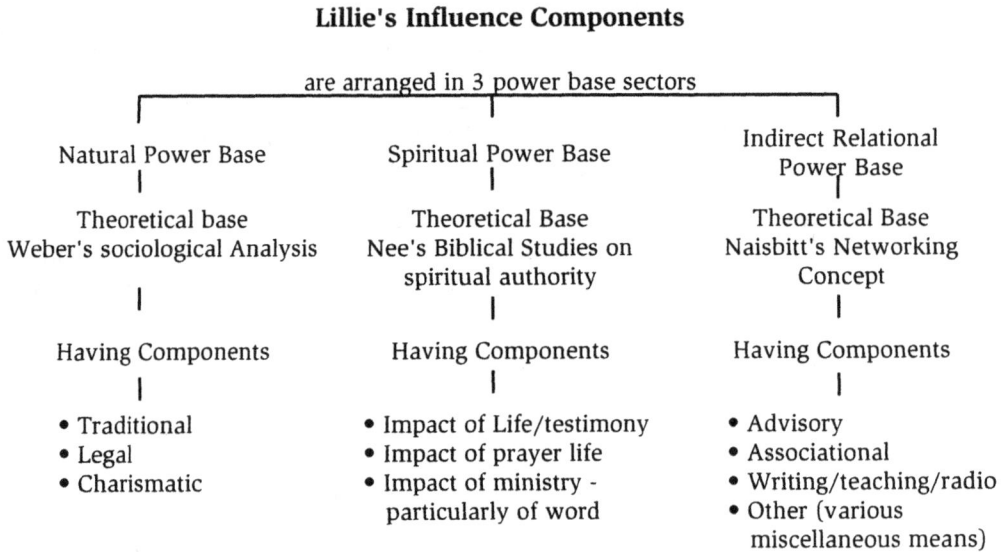

Lillie's Influence Components

are arranged in 3 power base sectors

Natural Power Base	Spiritual Power Base	Indirect Relational Power Base
Theoretical base Weber's sociological Analysis	Theoretical Base Nee's Biblical Studies on spiritual authority	Theoretical Base Naisbitt's Networking Concept
Having Components	Having Components	Having Components
• Traditional • Legal • Charismatic	• Impact of Life/testimony • Impact of prayer life • Impact of ministry - particularly of word	• Advisory • Associational • Writing/teaching/radio • Other (various miscellaneous means)

Explanation of Lillie's Diagram – The Standard Plot

Lillie divided a circular plot into three major power base sectors. Each sector was a "pie slice" of the total. Lillie assigned smaller pieces of the pie in a sector to a component. He then constructed concentric circles beginning with the center of the diagram. Each circle represents a level of influence: small group, community, regional, inter-regional, national, and international. He used these as his influence groups. However, various cultures may well use other categories as long as the groups are arranged from smallest to largest working from the inside of the pie to the outside.

Lillie looked at a component in a sector and asked at what level (influence group concentric circle) the trainee was influencing using that component. He darkened the intersection of the concentric circle representing the influence group and the arc of the sector component. If a component didn't apply he left it blank. The end result is a profile of darkened sectors representing the highest level of influence for each applicable sector component.

Other Plots

McConnell, et. al., in Papua New Guinea, used the plot to show progressive development of sphere of influence. They correlated the circular plot with the LSP time-line development phases of a trainee. For each development phase they put the Roman Numeral of the phase in the proper cross-sector. The resulting profile showed gains and/or losses of sphere of influence with time. Dennis Teague, a missionary to France, applied the concept to analysis of secular influence by radically changing the sector components. Still others doing strategic planning applied the concept on a corporate basis to a mission organization.

Map of Antioch, Cyprus and Asia Minor

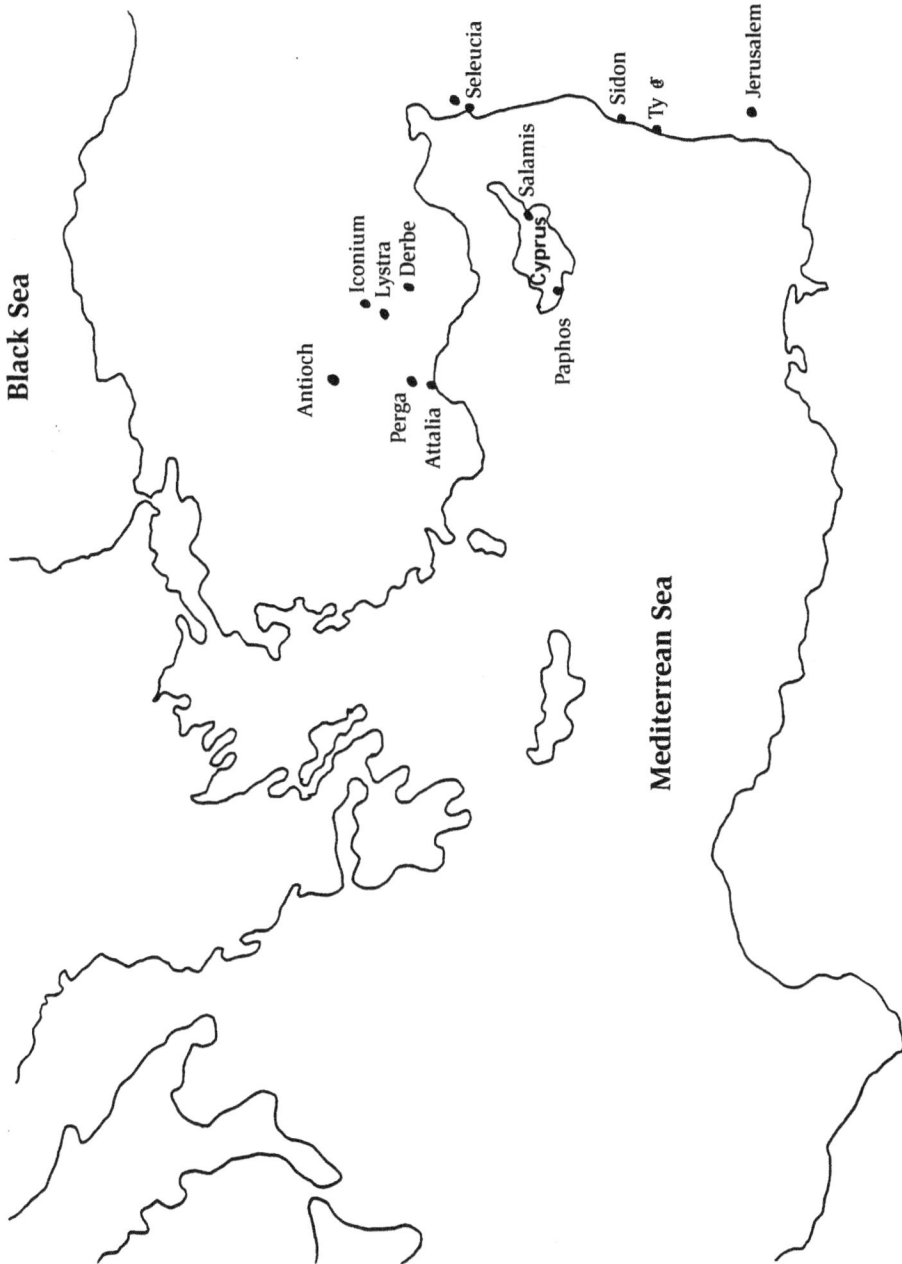

Black Sea

Mediterrean Sea

Antioch

Iconium
Lystra
Derbe

Perga
Attalia

Salamis

Cyprus

Paphos

Seleucia

Sidon
Ty &

Jerusalem

Bibliography

Bauckham, Richard J.
1979   "Barnabas in Galatians" *Journal for the Study of the New Testament* 2:61-70.

Blake, Robert R. and Mouton, Jane Srygley
1964   "*The Managerial Grid; Key Orientations for Achieving Production through People.* Houston: Gulf Publishing Company.

Bruce, F. F.
1954   *Commentary on the Book of the Acts.* Grand Rapids, Michigan: William B. Eerdmans Publishing Company; reprinted, 1974.

Cave, William
1840   "The Life of Saint Barnabas the Apostle." In *Lives of the Most Eminent Fathers of the Church That Flourished in the First Four Centuries;* vol. 1, revised by Henry Cary, pp. 90-105. Oxford: J. Vincent.

Clinton, James Robert
1985   *Spiritual Gifts.* Alberta, Can: Horizon House Publishers.

1979   "Prayer, Recrudescence, and the Cross-fertilization Effect. (Some Insights from Jonthan Edwards and the Prayer Concert)" Pasadena: School of World Mission. Unpublished paper for the course, The American Church and World Mission.

1984   *Leadership Emergence Theory.* Altadena: Barnabas Resources.

Dale, Robert D.
1979   "Barnabas: Hidden Leader of the New Testament." In *Leadership Profiles from Bible Personalities*, Ernest E. Mosley, compiler, pp. 102-114. Nashville, Tennessee: Broadman Press.

Donaldson, James
1874   *The Apostolical Fathers: A Critical Account of Their Genuine Writing and of Their Doctrines.* London: MacMillan.

Filson, Floyd F.
1940   *Pioneers of the Primitive Church.* New York: The Abingdon Press.

Flynn, Leslie B.
1974   *Nineteen Gifts of the Spirit.*Wheaton, Illinois: Victor Books.

Foggie, Charles H.
1980   "Barnabas and Paul or a Pair of Powerful Preachers" *The AME Zion Quarterly Review* 92 (3, October):21-26., William Mordaunt

1912   *The Acts of the Apostles.* Oxford: Clarendon Press.

Goodspeed, E. J.
1942   *A History of Early Christian Literature.* Chicago: The University of Chicago Press.

Gunther, John J.
1982   "The Association of Mark and Barnabas with Egyptian Christianity" *The Evangelical Quarterly,* part 1, 54 (October-December):218-233.

1983   "The Association of Mark and Barnabas with Egyptian Chriatianity" *The Evangelical Quarterly,* part 2, 55 (January):21-29.

Havelock,Ronald G.
1973   *The Change Agents Guide to Innovation in Education.* Englewood Cliffs, N.J.: Educational Technology Publications.

Jacobs, H. E.
1957   "Barnabas." In *The International Standard Bible Encyclopedia.* vol. I. James Orr et   al., ed. Grand Rapids: William B. Eerdmans Publishing Company.

Knox, Wilfred L.
1925   *St. Paul and the Church of Jerusalem.* Cambridge: University Press.

Roberson, A. T.
1922   *Types of Preachers in the New Testament.* New York: George Doran Company.

Ryley, G. Buchanan
1893   *Barnabas or the Great Renuncaition.* London: The Religious Tract Society.

Schaller, Lyle E.
1972   *The Change Agent*. Nashville: Abingdon Press.

Strong, James
1890   *The Exhaustive Concordance of the Bible*. New York: Abingdon Press.

Stroyer, M. J.
1962   "Barnabas." In *The Interpreter's Dictionary of the Bible*, vol. I. George Arthur   Buttrick, ed., pp. 356-57. New York: Abingdon Press.

Teague, Dennis
1983   "The Gift of Exhortation." Pasadena: School of World Mission, Fuller Theological Seminary. Unpublished portion of a programmed text dealing with Barnabas and the gift of exhortation.

Tippett, A. R.
1967   *Solomon Islands Christianity*. New York: Friendship Press.

Truett, George W.
1915   "A New Testament Good Man." In *We Would See Jesus; And Other Sermons*, J. B.   Cranfill, compiler, pp. 76-91. New York: Fleming H. Revell Company.

Wagner, C. Peter
1979   *Your Spiritual Gifts Can Help Your Church Grow*. Glendale: Regal Books.

Weiss, Johannes
1937   *History of Primitive Christianity*, vol. I. New York: Wilson-Erikson.

Glossary of Terms Used In This Booklet

Term	Definition
Afterglow	The sixth and final developmental stage in the generalized time line describing the time in a leader's development when the leader sees the fruit of a life-time of ministry and growth and has a period of mature celebration and indirect influence at broadest levels.
Apostleship	A spiritual gift which refers to a special leadership capacity in which one exerts influence over others so as to establish new local churches and new works needed to enhance the spread of Christianity. Further, this gift functions to guide these new works in their foundational stages.
Boundary Condition	A phrase used to describe the special processing that God uses to transition a leader from one sub-phase or phase of development to another.
Conflict Item	A special type of crisis process item seen often in the ministry maturing development stage in which the leader faces opposition and learns lessons in horizontal relationships.
Contextual Items	Refers to a class of process items referring to local, national and international factors of the historical setting in which the leader operates. These major historical dynamics will directly affect a leader's development as well as tasks, roles, etc.
Convergence	The fifth developmental stage in the generalized time line describing the time in a leader's development when the leader is moved by God into a role which matches his/her gift-mix, and experience, and temperament, so that the ministry output is maximized.
Conversion Item	A process item which refers to the study of conversion in the life of the leader in order to correlate the salvation experience with later ministry trends.
Crisis Item	A category of process items referring to those special intense situations of pressure in human situations which are used by God to test and teach dependence on God.

Term	Definition
Divine Contact	A person whom God brings to a leader at a leader at a crucial moment in a development phase in order to accomplish one or more of the following (or a related function): affirm leadership potential, encourage leadership potential, give guidance on a special issue, give insights which broaden the leader, challenge the leader Godward, open a door to ministry opportunity.
Evangelism	A spiritual gift defined as the capacity to confront people publicly and privately through various communicative methods with the message of salvation in Christ so as to see them respond by taking initial steps in Christian discipleship.
Family Process Item	A process item which refers to significant situations, events and personalities that occur in the early family life of a leader which help mold character, perspectives, abilities, etc. of the person and which play a significant influence on the exercise of leadership in convergence.
Gift-mix	A term coined by Dr. C. Peter Wagner in his book *Your Spiritual Gifts Can Help Your Church Grow* which refers to the cluster of spiritual gifts a leader demonstrates in his/her ministry.
Giving	A spiritual gift defined as the capacity to give liberally to meet the needs of others and yet to do so with a purity of motive which senses that the giving is a simple sharing of that which God has provided.
Goodwin's Expectation Principle	A generalization observed by Goodwin in his leadership booklet, *The Effective Leader* which states that a potential leader tends to rise to the level of genuine expectancy of a leader whom he/she respects.
Information Distribution Principle	A generalization observed in the historical expansion of the Christian movement which says that wide dissemination of facts about movements of God or God's increased recrudescence efforts greatly increases the rate of recrudescence and ultimately generates more movements.
Inner-life Growth	The second developmental stage in the generalized time line describing the time in a leader's development when God is focusing on developing inner character.

Term	Definition
Integrity Check	A special kind of process testing which God uses to evaluate heart-intent and which uses as a springboard to an expanded sphere of influence.
Leadership Backlash	A process item describing the reactions of followers, other leaders within the group, Christians outside the group or other opposition who react to a course of action because of the various ramifications that arise because of it.
Life Maturing	The fourth developmental stage in the generalized time line describing the time in a leader's development when the leader has identified and is using his/her gift-mix with power. There is mature fruitfulness. God is working through the leader using imitation modeling (Heb 13:7,8) and the life as well as giftedness. It is during this period that maturity processing deepens. Isolation, crises, literary factors, and a sense of destiny take on new meaning.
Managerial Grid	A graphic technique proposed by Blake and Mouton which analyzes, attempts to measure, and displays a given leader's composite leadership style of concern for production and concern for people.
Mentoring	A process in which a person with a serving, giving, encouraging attitude (the mentor) sees leadership potential in a still-to-be-developed person (the futuree or protégé or mentoree) and is able to promote or otherwise significantly influence the futuree along to the realization of potential.
Mercy	A spiritual gift referring to the capacity both to feel sympathy with those in need (especially those suffering and miserable) and to manifest this sympathy in some practical helpful way with a cheerful spirit so as to encourage and help those in need.
Ministry Maturing	The third stage in the generalized time line describing the time in a leader's development when the emerging leader learns major lessons about ministry. Ministry process items become prominent. Relationship lessons are increasingly learned. Power lessons become important. Spiritual authority takes on new significance.

Term	Definition
Ministry Task	A special process item defined as an assignment from God which primarily tests a person's faithfulness and obedience but often also allows use of ministry gifts in the context of a task which has closure, accountability, and evaluation.
ML 530	A course taught at the School of World Mission at Fuller Theological Seminary which deals with leadership emergence theory.
Obedience Check	Refers to that special category of process item in which God tests personal response to revealed truth in the life of a person.
Power Encounter	A term describing a climatic confrontation between God and other spiritual beings in which the human participants are made aware of God's superiority. A.R. Tippett, in his book *Solomon Island Christianity*, describes the concept.
Process Item	Leadership selection process items are those providential events, people, circumstances, special interventions, inner-life lessons and/or anything which God uses in the leadership selection process of a person to indicate leadership potential, to develop that potential, to confirm appointment to a role/responsibility and to move the leader along to God's appointed ministry level for the realized potential.
Pro-grammed Instruction	A form of self-study materials in which the text acts as a teacher and the reader acts as a learner. The instruction is carefully defined and sequentially ordered to provide the learner with a self-validating learning experience.
Sense of Destiny	A special process item describing a unique awe-inspiring experience or the accumulative effect of a series of experiences in which God reveals himself to an obedient surrendered believer in order to inspire/lead that person on to accomplish something special in his/her lifetime.
Sovereign Foundations	The first developmental stage in the generalized time line describing the time in a leader's development when God is sovereignly working through family, contextual background, etc. in the life of the individual. Personality characteristics and experiences both good and bad will all be used by God later for his purposes.

Term	Definition
Sphere of Influence	A phrase describing the totality of people being influenced by a leader and for whom a leader will give an account to God. The totality of people can be further refined to mean individuals or groups of people being directly influenced for which a leader has direct responsibility and for those people who are indirectly influenced by that leader.
Spiritual Authority	A phase describing a major power base from which a biblical leader operates to influence people. It is described as the characteristic of a God-anointed leader which rests upon clear evidence that Jesus speaks and acts through the leader's life and ministry, which relates to the influence the leader has on followers for their good, which is measured by the degree to which believers are yielding and responsive to the leader's persuasive influence (since the ultimate decision to obey from the heart rests with the believer), and which brings about spiritual maturity in those so influenced.
Spiritual Formation	A concept identified in training theory in Fred Holland's doctoral dissertation at the School of World Mission and which I have defined as the development of the inner-life of a person of God so that the person experiences more of God, reflects more God-like characteristics in personality and in everyday relationships, and increasingly knows the power and presence of God in ministry.
Spiritual Gift	Defined as a unique capacity given by the Holy Spirit to each believer for service in connection with the church in order to cause the church to progress quantitatively and/or qualitatively and/or organically.
Teaching	A spiritual gift defined as the capacity to instruct, explain to expose Biblical truth in such a way as to cause believers in a church to understand the biblical truth and to acquire the truth for their own use.
Word Check	A special case of the general word factor process item which tests a leader's ability to understand or receive a word from God personally and to see it worked out in life.

BARNABAS PUBLISHERS

BARNABAS PUBLISHER'S MINI CATALOG

Approaching the Bible With Leadership Eyes: An Authoratative Source for Leadership Findings — Dr. J. Robert Clinton

Barnabas: Encouraging Exhorter — Dr. J. Robert Clinton & Laura Raab

Boundary Processing: Looking at Critical Transitions Times in Leader's Lives — Dr. J. Robert Clinton

Connecting: The Mentoring Relationships You Need to Succeed in Life — Dr. J. Robert Clinton

The Emerging Leader — Dr. J. Robert Clinton

Fellowship With God — Dr. J. Robert Clinton

Finishing Well — Dr. J. Robert Clinton

Figures and Idioms (Interpreting the Scriptures: Figures and Idioms) — Dr. J. Robert Clinton

Focused Lives Lectures — Dr. J. Robert Clinton

Gender and Leadership — Dr. J. Robert Clinton

Having A Ministry That Lasts: By Becoming a Bible Centered Leader — Dr. J. Robert Clinton

Hebrew Poetry (Interpreting the Scriptures: Hebrew Poetry) — Dr. J. Robert Clinton

A Short **History of Leadership Theory** — Dr. J. Robert Clinton

Isolation: A Place of Transformation in the Life of a Leader — Shelley G. Trebesch

Joseph: Destined to Rule — Dr. J. Robert Clinton

The Joshua Portrait — Dr. J. Robert Clinton and Katherine Haubert

Leadership Emergence Theory: A Self Study Manual For Analyzing the Development of a Christian Leader — Dr. J. Robert Clinton

Leadership Perspectives: How To Study The Bible for Leadership Insights — Dr. J. Robert Clinton

Coming to Some Conclusions on **Leadership Styles** — Dr. J. Robert Clinton

Leadership Training Models — Dr. J. Robert Clinton

The Bible and **Leadership Values:** A Book by Book Analysis— Dr. J. Robert Clinton

The Life Cycle of a Leader: Looking at God's Shaping of A LeaderTowards An Eph. 2:10 Life — Dr. J. Robert Clinton

Listen Up Leaders! — Dr. J. Robert Clinton

The Mantle of the Mentor — Dr. J. Robert Clinton

Mentoring Can Help—Five Leadership Crises You Will Face in the Pastorate For Which You Have Not Been Trained — Dr. J. Robert Clinton

Mentoring: Developing Leaders... Without Adding More Programs — Dr. J. Robert Clinton

The Mentor Handbook: Detailed Guidelines and Helps for Christian Mentors and Mentorees — Dr. J. Robert Clinton

Moses Desert Leadership—7 Macro Lessons

Parables—Puzzles With A Purpose (Interpreting the Scriptures: Puzzles With A Purpose) — Dr. J. Robert Clinton

Paradigm Shift: God's Way of Opening New Vistas To Leaders — Dr. J. Robert Clinton

A Personal Ministry Philosophy: One Key to Effective Leadership — Dr. J. Robert Clinton

Reading on the Run: Continuum Reading Concepts — Dr. J. Robert Clinton

Samuel: Last of the Judges & First of the Prophets–A Model For Transitional Times — Bill Bjoraker

Selecting and Developing Those Emerging Leaders — Dr. Richard W. Clinton

Social Base Processing: The Home Base Environment Out of Which A Leader Works — Dr. J. Robert Clinton

Starting Well: Building A Strong Foundation for a Life Time of Ministry — Dr. J. Robert Clinton

Strategic Concepts: That Clarify A Focused Life – A Self Study Guide — Dr. J. Robert Clinton

The Making of a Leader: Recognizing the Lessons & Stages of Leadership Development — Dr. J. Robert Clinton

Time Line —Small Paper (What it is & How to Construct it) — Dr. J. Robert Clinton

Time Line: Getting Perspective—By Using Your Time-Line, Large Paper — Dr. J. Robert Clinton

Ultimate Contribution — Dr. J. Robert Clinton

Unlocking Your Giftedness: What Leaders Need to Know to Develop Themselves & Others — Dr. J. Robert Clinton

A **Vanishing Breed:** Thoughts About A Bible Centered Leader & A Life Long Bible Mastery Paradigm — Dr. J. Robert Clinton

The Way To Look At Leadership (How To Look at Leadership) — Dr. J. Robert Clinton

Webster-Smith, Irene: An Irish Woman Who Impacted Japan (A Focused Life Study) — Dr. J. Robert Clinton

Word Studies (Interpreting the Scriptures: Word Studies) — Dr. J. Robert Clinton

(Book Titles are in Bold and Paper Titles are in Italics with Sub-Titles and Pre-Titles in Roman)

BARNABAS   PUBLISHERS

Unique Leadership Material that will help you answer the question:
"What legacy will you as a leader leave behind?"

"The difference between leaders and followers is perspective. The difference
between leaders and effective leaders is better perspective."
Barnabas Publishers has the materials that will help you find that
better perspective and a closer relationship with God.

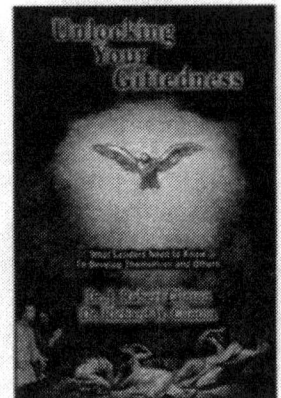

www.ingramcontent.com/pod-product-compliance
Lightning Source LLC
Chambersburg PA
CBHW081633040426
42449CB00014B/3294